ON THE
Wings OF
Eagles

A True Story of Faith, Hope, and Love

Lance and Robin Croom

OnThe Wings of Eagles

Lance and Robin Croom

© 2016

ISBN 978-0692744321

Eagles Wings Publishing

EMAIL THE AUTHOR at:

onthewingsofeagles1@gmail.com

Printed in the United States of America

Table of Contents

This book is dedicated to our parents,

Henry and Sylvia Mitchell

and Shirley Croom

as they rest in glory

September 17, 2001

I don't understand Lord! *How can you give us a ministry that takes both of us, and how can you give us a vision for this business, then take my husband away from me?* I don't understand! *I don't want my testimony to be how to get over losing your spouse,* I DON'T WANT THAT TO BE MY TESTIMONY LORD! *But, I'm not telling you what to do.*

Praying to God through uncontrollable tears, from months of frustration, and a weariness that only comes from pure exhaustion, I released it all. I was physically, mentally, and spiritually exhausted. In spite of my feelings of total abandonment, loneliness, despair, and dread at what was in-store for me, something deep inside me stirred. It was the spirit of God. It was like a calm resolve came over me, and the next words out of my mouth were...

But, whatever road I have to travel, I will go. And whatever path I have to take, I will take it. I will serve you Lord! I will praise you Lord, and I will continue to love you Lord!

It was at this point of total surrender to my sovereign God, relinquishing my will for his good, perfect, and acceptable will, that I heard the loving voice of God! He said these words to me...Robin, that is not going to be your testimony, I'm just working with him (speaking of my husband Lance).

1

I cried harder, but this time out of an attitude of total thankfulness and praise. I thanked God for loving me, caring for me and not forgetting me. The next item on the agenda was to quickly go and share with Lance the word that I had gotten from God.

Please take a journey with Lance and me through the pages of our life; beginning with our childhood, and ending with where we are today. We will openly share our challenges, defeats, triumphs, and failures. We pray that our experiences in life and with God will both encourage you and cause you to want to get closer to Jesus. Our journey is paved with faith, hope, and love. Because of this journey our lives have forever been changed, never to be the same again. God has prepared us from the day we were born to share ourselves with you. We hope as you read on that you will come to understand that God is preparing you as well. God is preparing you for something great. God is preparing you to fulfill your purpose that he has pre-ordained for your life! God has a plan for you too, but the road to your destiny may take you to places that you never thought you would travel.

Chapter One

Growing Up

(Lance)

Growing up in Detroit during the turbulent '60s was rough. I had to be tough to survive the inner-city streets.

During that era the black population started a significant growth spurt in a predominantly white city. In 1950 blacks made up 16.1% of Detroit's population, 1960 28.9% and 1970 44.5%. Many white people did not take kindly to the change, which caused racial tension and even violence. Some of the racists were white cops working the streets in groups of four, known as the "Tac Squad" or "Big Four." They targeted blacks and arrested them legally or illegally. During some of those arrests blacks were roughed-up or even worse, shot. Sadly, some died at the hands of white officers causing blacks to riot in protest.

Detroit had another problem too. Drug trafficking became a big business (mostly heroin and marijuana). Both white and black drug pushers moved on the streets and the skin color of their customers did not matter, they would sell to whomever wanted to buy. Some of the dealers claimed their own territory. Many times when another dealer infringed on their turf violence occurred, even to the point of death. Because there were so many senseless killings, Detroit became known as the "Murder Capital" of the country!

Violence was prevalent everywhere I went. I learned at a very young age that if you showed fear on the inner-city streets (also known as the "hood") it was a sign of weakness. If you did not fight to keep your lunch money you would lose it. I stood my ground but it came with a price. I had lots of fistfights. I became a 'Tough Little Dude." Although I was not considered a "big kid" (short and on the skinny side) I didn't back down to anyone! As I walked the streets of Detroit I developed a thick skin, and there was a confident edge and (cool) swagger about me.

During my childhood my family did not have much money so in order to buy anything, I had to work for it. As young as seven years old I did whatever I could for a few bucks. I raked leaves, shoveled snow and even swept out shops in my neighborhood. My strong work ethic came from my brothers Tony and Michael, the two eldest in my family, respectively six and five years older than me. Every time I asked either of them for money or to buy me something they refused. Their reason was that they did not want to handicap me by giving handouts, which would eventually spoil me. Instead, they taught me what to say to neighbors and shopkeepers to earn a few bucks. So, I approached everyone that I could for work. I loved having money in my pocket! So much so, I developed a reputation. I was known as the "Little Hustler."

For the most part the memories of my childhood are filled with happiness and fun times. I owe that to my mother, because even though we didn't have much materially, she showed us a lot of love. Our mom (widowed) raised us to be close to each other. We looked out for one another. After Tony and Michael, there came Yvonne, Gregory, me, then Norman. Seven and a half years separate the six of us from youngest to oldest. Eleven years later our youngest sister Patricia was born, a total of seven children.

Our mother taught us to judge a man not by the color of his skin but by the content of his character. She told us to not hate people but to love them. That was not an easy thing to do, being black and growing up in Detroit during a violent racist era, but it did help me get through those tough years and it has made me a better man today.

My mother was very intelligent and well read. She instilled in us the love of reading. I can remember her saying, "You can see the world through a book." Getting an education was highly encouraged in our family. My mother started college but because of getting married at a very young age and starting a family right away she did not finish. There was a lot of love in our home. My mother had a "huge heart" she would give to those in need even when we did not have enough for ourselves. Her compassion and words of wisdom were instrumental in the development of the man that I am today.

When I say that our family didn't have much money, I mean we were poor, and I do not mean lower middle-class type of poor, I mean "third-world poor." My siblings and I were raised on the east side of Detroit in dilapidated government projects, or the "slums" as referred to by some. I give my mother a lot of credit; she did the best that she could under the circumstances.

My father died of leukemia when I was one and a half years old, so that made things very difficult for her. She never remarried. My mother did not work when I was young. We survived on a small monthly social security check from my father's death benefits, and government aid for supplemental food.

There were times when we did not have any food to eat nor heat during the harsh Michigan winters. I can remember one freezing cold night shivering in bed while huddling with Gregory and Norman to keep warm. Gregory wet the bed, and I did too. In any other scenario being peed on would have made me sick, but because it was so cold (oddly) I welcomed the warmth that it brought. Even though the warm sensation did not last long before the wetness became cold, I enjoyed the moment of comfort. The mattress that I shared with my siblings was covered in urine stains due to the fact that my mother could not afford to replace it.

The projects were notorious for bedbugs. They would bite us all the time, keeping us from sleeping through the night. Although my mother tried to keep a clean home we had cockroaches too, another common insect related to living in government projects.

I am amazed at how well my siblings and I turned out considering the conditions in which we were raised. I give God all the credit! My grandfather (on my mother's side) was a Baptist minister. He and my grandmother prayed for us regularly. We used to attend their church most Sundays. One of my fondest childhood memories was attending vacation bible school at Russell Street Baptist Church.

Most of my friends never made it out of the ghetto. The majority of them are either deceased from drug related violence or they overdosed on heroin. Some wound up in prison for many years, even life-sentences. Looking back on my childhood, I believe that my grandparents' prayers are what made the difference. Strange as it may seem, I can remember making a vow, about the age of four, that if given an opportunity I would do better.

Our home in the projects was amongst a row of three (attached) single-family houses. We stayed there until it was accidentally burned down. Christmas Eve day (1962), when I was six years old, my mother went out to do some morning errands. She left Tony in charge of Gregory, Norman, and me (Yvonne and Michael were not home at the time). Tony (twelve years old) did not want to watch us, he wanted to hang out with his friends. So, once my mom went out the front door, Tony immediately went out the back door.

There was no heat in our apartment and we were freezing! Gregory had an idea of how to get us warm. During those years Tony and Michael had an early morning job unloading trucks at the Eastern Market. Sometimes, if my mother was not home or if it was very cold, they would bring Yvonne, Gregory, Norman, and me with them. In order to keep warm in the wintertime (while at work), Tony and Michael would make a fire in a steal garbage container. We watched them put scraps of wood in the container, pour kerosene on top, and light it with a match.

Well, on that cold Christmas Eve morning, Gregory asked me to help him roll in a steal garbage container filled with trash from outside into our living room. I did. There was no kerosene or matches in our home, so Gregory rolled up a brown paper bag walked over to the gas stove and turned on a burner. He lit the paper in hopes of making it to the container before the flame reached his hand. Norman (five years old), wanting to be part of the action, yelled, "I want to do it!" He reached up and took the lit paper from Gregory. The paper bag went up in flames fast, singeing Norman's fingers, causing him to drop it on the floor next to our old worn-out couch (four feet short of the container). Whoosh! Just like that the couch went up in flames and it was only a matter of seconds before the living room was ablaze. Gregory, Norman and I stood frozen in place amazed at how quickly the fire turned into a fascinating inferno! Were it not for our elderly next-door neighbor, Mr. Patterson, who was like a surrogate grandfather, charging in and rescuing us we probably would have died in there.

With nowhere else to go we moved in with my grandmother (my grandfather had passed away the year before of congestive heart failure). A couple of good things came out of our home burning down. Thankfully my grandmother lived in a nice neighborhood towards the west side of Detroit, which meant no more "slums!" More importantly, her house always had enough food, heat, and there were no bedbugs, cockroaches or urine stained mattresses.

My grandmother rented a flat in a three-bedroom brick two-story house (two separate residences shared by a common front door). Simply put, she lived in the upstairs half of a house and another tenant lived in the bottom half, each with their own (inner) door. Three of my aunts and two uncles lived there, too. My mother was the eldest of thirteen, couple that with being only seventeen years old when pregnant with Tony, my aunts and uncles that we moved in with were only ten to fifteen years older than me. Needless to say, because the seven of us moved in with the six of them, in a fairly small apartment, we were packed in like sardines! For the most part all of us got along well considering the extremely tight living conditions but I sensed that my aunts resented us moving there. At times they were mean to my siblings and me.

In a span of two months my mother was able to save up enough money to put down a deposit and pay rent on a flat of our own. Thankfully the place was also on the west side of town. It was nice having our "own space" again!

My grandmother decided to use some of my grandfather's death benefits as a down payment to purchase a huge six-bedroom (two-story) house on the Westside in a middle-class neighborhood. Three of my aunts and two uncles that were living in my grandmother's flat moved there as well. It was a beautiful home! My grandmother asked my mother if she wanted to move in and help pay the hefty mortgage. So, nine months after having our own space my family moved to 1746 W. Boston Street. This time there was plenty of room for all thirteen of us.

In a relatively short period of time I went from poverty-stricken projects clear across Detroit to a fairly well-to-do-area.

I have many fond memories of living on W. Boston Street. Holidays were always fun. Thanksgiving and Christmas were especially enjoyable. The women of the house cooked a delicious meal and lots of it, too. We decorated the house for Christmas including a full size tree in our living room. Everyone sang Christmas carols, drank eggnog and laughed a lot. I remember practicing my lines for our church's annual Christmas play.

Although we lived in a very spacious house (unlike the small flat that we all shared previously), my aunts were still resentful of us living with them. The longer that my siblings and I lived on W. Boston Street, the meaner they were towards us. It got to the point where I did not feel welcome in my own home. Often I would stay away from the house all day just to get away from them. In the summertime I went outside from seven in the morning until the evening as many times as I could. The rule in our home was that we needed to be in the house when the streetlights came on, or at least on the front porch.

Two years after moving to W. Boston Street I witnessed Gregory die tragically at nine years of age. The two of us along with Norman were playing in an alley around the corner from our house. We saw a slow moving Mac truck (eighteen wheeler) pulling a cargo trailer. The driver seemed to be looking for a place to park. Since the truck was moving so slowly we decided to jump on the back of the trailer out of the driver's view. The truck made a stop then proceeded to back up along a curb; Gregory fell off hitting the back of his head hard on the pavement. Stunned, he just laid there. As if it were in slow motion I watched the tires of the truck run over him. In a panic Norman and I ran home to tell our mother what had happen. I will always remember her reaction of disbelief, "No! No! God, no!"

Gregory's death remains a vivid memory. Losing my older brother left a void in me for many years. Recently, Tony and I were reminiscing about him. He said, "Gregory was like an old-soul and wise beyond his years. He went through a lot at a very young age." Tony mentioned the time when Gregory was four years old, he reached to the top of the stove and pulled down a pan of hot grease on himself, severely burning his neck and chest. Tony further stated, "God was being merciful by calling him home early because he had suffered enough in this life."

Gregory was always protective of his younger brothers. He would have fought to the death to protect Norman and me, if necessary. I looked up to him. He was kind-hearted and wise. I remember wanting to beat up one of Gregory's friends because the girl that I liked did not like me in the same way that she liked him. So, I challenged this kid to a fight. Gregory intervened; he told me that my behavior was silly (wanting to beat up some guy because a girl didn't like me); I backed down after that.

Although W. Boston Street was in a nice residential area it was only two blocks from a ghetto (inner-city) area. In my youth I spent a lot of time on the streets of Detroit. Although I was able to buy things because of earning money from various types of (odd) jobs, I stole things from time-to-time, mostly candy and soda pop. At times I was wayward. I had a really good understanding of right and wrong but I stole things anyway. I can remember getting into trouble for going into a neighbor's garage and taking empty soda pop bottles to redeem for money. I got a whooping for it and never did that again!

My brothers Tony and Michael were known on the streets as being tough and they were respected for that. They taught me how to handle myself in a fistfight. It was feast or famine on the streets. If you didn't fight for your rights, then you would always be a target. I had too much pride to back down from a challenge, plus my competitive nature wouldn't let me. It did not take long before the guys in the "hood" stopped picking on me because word got out that I could fight. I did not back down to anyone! When it became known that I was a "tough little dude" my walk got a lot more swagger!

Michael always had lots of girlfriends. When I was seven years old he taught me how to meet girls. He was my role model and I tried to emulate him. Both Michael and Tony always dressed-to-impress the ladies! In the '60s being "cool" took on a whole new meaning. Tony and Michael grew out their hair to straighten it (chemical treatment process), wore silk shirts with gabardine slacks and alligator skin shoes. In the wintertime they styled a turtleneck under a cashmere (V-neck) sweater. I could not wait for the day when I would be old enough to wear cool clothes, too!

The '60s is also known for Motown, smooth and cool music with an unforgettable beat, and I lived in "Motor City" (hence the name) where the record label was birthed. Many well-known artists got recognized through Motown Records. The Temptations, Four Tops, The Supremes, Stevie Wonder,

Commodores, and The Pointer Sisters just to name a few. I grew-up in the best era of music ever!

On the inner-city streets of Detroit, I had it all going on; toughness, swagger, and I was always smooth with the girls. I strutted while snapping my fingers to a Motown beat and whistled the melody.

"Little Hustler" became my M.O. in every facet of life. I grew up fast! When I was eight years old I started experimenting with sex by making-out with girls. At age nine I learned how to gamble by pitching quarters and rolling dice on the streets. At age eleven I experienced sexual intercourse for the first time. I became infatuated with chasing girls! It became a hobby because I found self-esteem in my ability to have sex with many girls. Knowing that I had a charming personality I talked with as many girls as I could. From age eight to twelve I started getting chubby, so I started building muscles by doing push-ups and sit-ups. By the time that I turned thirteen I was buffed at five foot eight inches tall and one hundred fifty pounds – "black stallion"!

By this time my stealing habits escalated to wine and beer. I wanted to bring alcohol to the basement parties that my friends had every Friday and Saturday night. I didn't enjoy hard alcohol and neither beer nor wine appealed to me, but because all my friends were drinking, so did I. To fit in I decided to only drink the sweet tasting wine. I also picked up a bad habit of smoking cigarettes, a habit I would have for many years.

Although I was pretty smart I did not apply myself in school. In seventh grade I often skipped classes to hangout on the streets to gamble and hookup with girls. By eighth grade my desire to skip school increased and my mother became very concerned about the path that I was on. In addition, my mother knew that I tried to emulate my brother, Michael as much as I could. He had just been released from prison (a two-year sentence) for breaking and entering. Soon after his freedom he moved in with our Uncle Carl in Los Angeles, in hopes of getting a fresh start on life.

My cousin, Juliette (whom I refer to as one of my aunts because she is closer to my mother's age than mine) spoke on the phone with my mother about me moving to Los Angeles to live with her family. She said that the change in environment might be what I needed to become motivated in school. My mother agreed. We planned to move while I was on summer break in-between eighth and ninth grade. Although I did not want to move from Detroit I liked the idea of my brother, Michael, living close by.

My Aunt Valerie (Val) caught wind of my upcoming move and suggested to my mother that I would benefit by moving in with her family in Riverside, California. By this time my brother, Norman, had already moved in with Aunt Val and Uncle Bennie. Norman was a good kid and did not get into trouble. He thought that moving there would provide a better opportunity to succeed in life than in Detroit. Also, he was close in age with our cousin, Victor (Aunt Val and Uncle Bennie's son).

My mother stuck with her original plan and sent me to live with Juliette. I traveled by air. Being it was my first flight the experience was very exciting! Once I arrived at Juliette's house (suitcases in hand) my second cousin, Rafael (Juliette's son)

informed me that the elders of their Jehovah Witne
that I could not stay with them because I w?
Witness, too.

That put me in an uncomfortable situation. ֽ
Michael (knowing my feelings were hurt) asked me if I w.
move in with him and Uncle Carl. I liked that idea! Word o₁
circumstance spread throughout the family. Aunt Val spoke with
my mother and said that because my uncle Carl and brother
Michael had busy schedules there would be little supervision for
me there. She said it would be like jumping from the frying pan
into the fire because I could get into as much trouble in Los
Angeles as I did in Detroit. My mother talked it over with
Michael and her brother Carl and decided it best that I move to
Riverside. In retrospect, that was the best decision. As for the
Jehovah Witness aspect of the situation, I say, "Praise Jesus"
because I do not know how things would have turned out if I
had stayed with Juliette.

So, I wound up moving in with Aunt Val, Uncle Bennie,
cousins Carmen (my age), Victor and Lisa (both younger than
me), and Norman.

Aunt Val loved me as much as my mother did. She had faith
in me and did not try to mold or change my ways. I have a lot of
respect for her and my mother, too. Both were great influences
in my life. Aunt Val and my mother had the same qualities.
They showed love to everyone and led by example. Both were of
strong character.

When arriving in Riverside I expected to see a river flowing
through the city (hence the name) but there was no body of

er to be found. There was just a dried up riverbed. I knew of e many lakes in Michigan and was disappointed that Riverside did not have at least one river. This part of Southern California is an hour east from the coast, hot and very dry.

Southern California was laid back and it took some getting used to. Also, Riverside, being a much smaller city than Detroit, did not compare to the fast paced lifestyle that this "Little Hustler" left behind.

I was bored! I spoke on the phone with my mother about once or twice a month and she wrote often. After my first eight months in Riverside I informed Aunt Val that I wanted to go back to Detroit. She knew that in time I would adjust to Southern California. Aunt Val made a deal with me, if I stayed in Riverside for at least fifteen months she would buy me a round-trip flight to Detroit. I kept to the deal and so did she. The following summer I went back to my grandmother's house and I was supposed to stay until school was to start. To my surprise I wound up leaving within ten days. Things were not the same as when I left and I was not the same person either. I felt as if I did not belong on the streets of Detroit anymore. Without realizing it I was adjusting to a Southern California lifestyle after-all. My trips to Detroit became less frequent throughout the years as I grew accustomed to living in Riverside, California.

Carmen, Victor, and Lisa were very smart (straight A) students, which triggered my competitive spirit to excel in school. I befriended some of Norman's friends in California. Carmen had sophisticated (stuffy) friends; they did not fit my cool style.

Norman wound up moving back to Detroit a year after I arrived. The change in environment in itself did not give him a better opportunity to succeed. In fact, the complete opposite occurred. His grades were slipping to the point that he received some failing grades. Continuation (special education) classes were recommended. In addition, Norman uncharacteristically got into trouble for fighting. Norman and I, along with some of our friends got into a fight with some guys in school. As teachers came to break it up we split but Norman did not run fast enough and got caught. After my Aunt Val received a phone call from the principal's office she decided that Norman might be better off finishing his education back in Detroit. She thought that maybe by Norman going back home he would turn his grades around for the better.

Most Southern California guys dressed in tee shirts, blue jeans, and sneakers. They looked at me as being different because I dressed sharply and I thought of myself as "all that" when it came to fashion. I was always a leader, never a follower. I stayed true to who I was, double knit pants, colorful shirts, polished shoes, and although Riverside does not get cold in the wintertime I still wore stylish sweaters. I always dressed-to-impress the ladies! That part of my life did not change in-spite of Southern California living.

Chapter Two

Growing Up

(Robin)

I reflect upon my early years in loving memory of my father, Henry Mitchell (1931 – 2011); mother, Sylvia (1932 – 2008); and brother, Craig (1961 – 2001).

Unlike Lance, my early years were not filled with hardship and challenge. If I was ever asked to sum up my childhood in one word it would be, "Blessed."

I had extraordinary parents! They raised my three brothers and me in a stable loving home. We did not want for anything. Our family was close and I could not have asked for a better upbringing.

Philadelphia, Pennsylvania is where I was born in 1957. Just prior to my birth my family was living in Virginia. My father, having joined the Army in 1948, was stationed at Fort Lee during the mid 1950s. My parents experienced lots of racist attitudes and behaviors. For that reason, my mother did not want me to be born in "the South". Both my mother and father were born in Philadelphia, and that was her preference for me too. So, when my mother was eight and a half months pregnant my father took time off from work and drove the family to my grandmother's house (on my mother's side). Within a couple of weeks, I arrived. Two weeks later my parents drove back to Virginia with a new addition to their family, me!

In October of 1957 my father's enlistment was coming to an end. He decided not to re-enlist with the Army but instead to transfer to the Air Force because of the special incentives that they were offering. It was a big decision on my dad's part because his new military base was clear across the USA in Riverside California.

I learned at a young age that being a military kid meant that my family might not stay in one place for very long. After I graduated from kindergarten, my dad received an order transferring him to Tachikawa Japan.

My family and I boarded the President Hoover passenger liner out of San Francisco and cruised across the Pacific Ocean. Through a six-year old's eyes, I remember the ship being huge! The trip took several weeks. To keep the passengers entertained during the long journey members of the ship's crew planned fun things for us to do. I participated in a children's "Dress Up Contest" and won first place! My mother creatively made a "Carmen Miranda" costume. Although Carmen was a native of Brazil she became a very popular entertainer in the USA during the 1940s. In her performances, she wore extravagant and colorful outfits reflecting Brazil's beauty. Her signature headpiece was a fruit-filled turban. With that in mind, my mother dressed me in a white halter-top and a bright multi-colored long skirt. That in itself did not win the competition for me but what she attached to my head did. My mother filled a turban with oranges, apples, pears, bananas and grapes! To this day I do not know how she kept the fruit from falling out. As a kid I loved the limelight and soaked up all the attention that the costume received. I thought that I was the bomb!

After arriving in Japan we moved into "Kanto Mura Family Housing Annex" located in Chofu, which is close to Tachikawa. My brothers and I had so much fun overseas. During the winter months we built snow igloos in the backyard of our home. There were plenty of snowball fights, too! When the weather heated up we cooled off in a community pool. Some of the Chofu vendors made money by selling rock candy to the United States military children through an opening at the bottom of a fence, which surrounded the housing complex. I always tried to pick the biggest piece!

The year after we moved to Japan "Shinkansen" (high-speed rail lines) opened for service in 1964. Their extremely fast train nicknamed "The Bullet" reached record-breaking speeds of up to 135 mph. Nowadays there are faster trains but back in the 1960s that was pretty amazing! The new rail line made traveling from one end of Japan to the other very convenient and began just nine days before Tokyo hosted the 1964 Summer Olympics. My family and I rode on "The Bullet" to attend some of the Olympic sporting events.

We experienced many other memorable moments during our three years overseas. I remember Meiji National Park being beautiful. Seemingly every floral color imaginable was there. The

Cherry Blossoms were spectacular! Buddha statutes and shrines were everywhere.

My parents were very sociable; they made many Japanese friendships that spanned over a lifetime. It did not take them long to pick up some of the Japanese language, my brothers and I, too. My father befriended Shigeo Nagashima of the Yomiuri Giants (1958-1974). He is considered by many to be the greatest player in the history of Nippon Baseball.

After I finished third grade my dad was transferred back to Riverside, California. Later that year my parents bought their first home, an L-shaped ranch-style house in a middleclass neighborhood, only fifteen miles from March Air Force Base. Surprisingly, my father did not receive any other orders to transfer out of Riverside. I was very fortunate to have spent the remainder of my childhood, adolescence and teen years in that home.

I loved growing up in Southern California with my brothers. Kenny was born three years before me, Wayne three years after me, and last but not least, Craig was born a couple of years after Wayne.

Kenny was very protective of Wayne, Craig, and me. As the older sibling of my two younger brothers I was also protective of them. We watched out for each other and always remained close. I have so much love for them!

Being the only girl and having three "extremely competitive" brothers turned me into a tomboy. I wanted to do everything that they did. I was not the "girly" type anyway, although I did have a couple of dolls. Not only did I take on any challenge that they gave me but I also challenged them, too.

We played tag, hide-and-go-seek, board games, cards, pick-up-sticks, marbles and jacks. I was the "Master" at jacks! The little red ball did not bounce all that high so we exchanged it with a golf ball. At the peak of my playing days I referred to myself as the "Queen" because I could scoop up twenty-five jacks with my right hand before the ball touched the floor a second time. No one could beat me! Many times I challenged my brothers to see who could climb a tree the fastest and also challenged them to many foot races, too. Most of the time I won because I was very fast!

We were truly blessed to have had the best mother and father. Whenever our parents went somewhere my brothers and I went, too. I do not remember ever having a babysitter. We did everything together as a family. Each year we went on at least one family vacation. Every three years we drove to Philadelphia, during the summer months, to visit family. A couple of times we went to Disneyland, which was only an hour away. Most Sunday afternoons we took a family drive to the countryside or the coast. Along the way we talked, sang songs and laughed a lot. Many times we would stop by A&W Root Beer for ice cream floats!

We always ate together as a family; soon after my father came home from work my mother called my brothers and me for dinner. She was a great cook! We enjoyed wonderful well-balanced meals. I ate whatever was served except for green peas and beets – yuck! My brothers did not like green peas, either. We would hide them under a pork chop bone or scatter them around our plate to make it look like we ate more than we did. Sometimes we would stuff our mouths full with peas then ask to be excused to use the bathroom to flush them down the toilet. Of course our parents knew, but they showed us grace.

Like a typical kid I did not like doing chores around the house but it was mandatory, my brothers had them, too. Washing dishes after dinner was the worst! We did not have a dishwashing machine in those days. I sure felt like a dishwashing machine after we ate a "big meal."

In our house my father set the rules. What he and my mother said was final! They said what they meant and did what they said. They were very fair but kids tend to push the envelope to see what they can get away with and I was no different. There were times when my mother repeatedly told me to clean my room but I didn't. Her last resort was, "You better get it done before your dad gets home!" That usually got my attention.

To the surprise of most people I tell; I never got spankings. Maybe it was because I was a girl, but then again, neither did Kenny. I was a sensitive child. The thought of my parents being displeased with me was enough for me to feel the necessary remorse for my errant actions. I wanted to please my mom and dad but as for my younger brothers that was another story. My dad did not allow my brothers to hit me even if I hit them first. Sometimes my brothers would aggravate or irritate me and on occasion I was known to ball-up my right hand into a fist and sock them dead in the middle of their backs! When they were very young they did not hit me back but as they got older Wayne and Craig did. When they retaliated like that I would run to my daddy crying and they got a spanking. I know it was not fair, but that was one of the perks of being a girl! Most of the time the spankings that they got were well deserved, so do not feel too bad for them.

As unusual as this may sound to some, as a teenager, I liked doing things with my parents. Not only that but I enjoyed sharing my mother and father with my friends. That was how I was raised – to share. Our home was filled with love and acceptance towards everyone. I was honored to be their daughter!

My mother worked very hard at keeping house. She chose to stay home to raise my brothers and me until I turned thirteen years old. By that time my dad retired from the Air Force and my parents opened a restaurant in San Bernardino, "Highland Haven BBQ," twenty minutes from Riverside. The business took up a lot of my parents' time, which considerably altered our family schedule, but we remained close despite the change. My brothers and I worked at the restaurant whenever we could, which meant after school and weekends. We worked there many hours during the summer months. The same loving ways that we experienced in our home transferred over to the cozy (family style) restaurant. The business attracted many repeat customers; most of them remained loyal for years.

I was blessed to have the "best mother" a girl could have. When I read verses from Proverbs 31 (NKJ) I am reminded of her:

10. Who can find a virtuous wife? For her worth is far above rubies.

11. The heart of her husband safely trusts her; so he will have no lack of gain.

12. She does him good and not evil all the days of her life.

20. She extends her hand to the poor, yes, she reaches out her hands to the needy.

26. She opens her mouth with wisdom, and on her tongue is the law of kindness.

27. She watches over the ways of her household.

28. Her children rise up and call her blessed: her husband also, and he praises her.

Just like the Proverbs 31 woman my mother sewed. She made pretty dresses for me. I can remember as young as five years old my mother coming home from the fabric store and soon afterwards I would have a colorful and stylish dress! She taught me how to sew, cook and bake. I did some "girly" stuff but when it came to hanging out with my brothers I was all "tomboy."

My mother was always there for my brothers and me no matter what challenges came our way. We knew that we could go to her for loving support. She was the ultimate caregiver; my brothers and I felt protected every time that we were around her. Our childhood photos, which included our mother, showed us wrapped around her legs. Wherever she went we went, too. I can remember one particular summer night, when my brothers and I were in our teens, we slept on the beach and our protective mother sat on a picnic table bench the entire night keeping a close eye on us. That example is one of many, which depicts my mother's nurturing ways. We always felt safe and loved when she was around.

My mother was meek and at the same time very wise. She regularly prayed for her family. Everyone loved her because she was fun, kind, caring, loving and compassionate. She was the nucleus that kept our closely-knit family intact. As I matured into the woman that I am today I have come to appreciate my mother's quiet strength and grace. Simply put – she was the best! I miss her.

Being the only daughter I was "daddy's little girl." We had a great father-daughter relationship. I just adored him! He was cool, wise, intelligent, dedicated and handsome. It was easy to admire him because he was a great example of the ultimate "man's-man."

He loved my mother and all his children. My dad was a great provider, too. He made sure that we were well taken care of. My father's leadership was from his heart. He treated all people with class and dignity. His character was commendable. Everyone that came to know my dad respected him.

He shared with me of the time (before I was born) when he was in the Korean War and taken as a POW. He escaped and survived two weeks behind enemy lines in sub-zero temperatures before making his way to a United States controlled territory. He avoided being recaptured by traveling at night and hiding during the day. That courageous act depicts my father's strong character. I am blessed; the same bloodline that flowed through his veins runs through mine. He was a great man and forever my hero!

My father got prostate cancer and in time it spread into his bones causing him a lot of pain. Since my mom had passed away my dad came to live with my husband and me. When he became too ill to care for himself, I cared for him. It was an honor and privilege to give to him, the last fifteen months of his life, what he had given to me all of my life! Love, care, compassion, and patience. It was hard to watch my dad suffer, but he died with the same strength and dignity that he lived with. When my father entered heaven, after eighty great years, I know he heard, "Well done my good and faithful servant!"

My mother was a cancer survivor. I vividly remember the dreaded phone call that came in October of 1979. Hearing concern in my mom's voice I knew something was wrong. She told me that she had found a lump in her breast and the doctor had informed her it was cancerous. That was a difficult time for our entire family. Throughout the chemo and radiation treatments my mother continued living with strength and grace. She remained upbeat during the long journey to recovery. Her inner-strength amazed me. My mother battled and won that fight. In the mid 1990s she developed diabetes and learned to live with that too, but other types of health complications that are associated with diabetes led to kidney failure and dialysis. In time she developed pneumonia ending her life at 75 years of age, but what I will remember is how she LIVED her life! My mom guarded her heart and didn't allow the enticements of the world to distract her focus from her family and the things of God. She was a phenomenal woman!

Craig got ill from a lung disorder (interstitial lung disease) in 1998. He then had a lung transplant but wound up dying three years later from the disease. He was a wonderful brother! Craig had a huge heart; people just loved being around him. He was fun too, the practical-joker of our family. Craig could make anyone laugh. Just being around him would lift your spirit. My brother became interested in fitness and health and started building his body. He entered and won several bodybuilding competitions. He was a "beast", but to me he embodied his nickname, "Teddy Bear." He was a successful entrepreneur, building his business "Tough Activewear" into a million-dollar venture. A silhouette of his physique became the company logo. Craig brought a new look into the industry of "work-out" wear in the early 1990s.

It was hard saying goodbye to my mother, father, and baby brother but knowing that we will be together again (in the presence of Jesus) helps lessen the pain of losing them. If I could share only one thought now it would be to love without regrets. Life is precious and it is short. Give all the love in your heart now while you can. *"Life is like the morning fog; it's here a little while, then it's gone."*

When I reflect over my childhood years, a smile fills my face and my heart is thankful! Thank you Lord.

Chapter Three

How We Met

(Robin)

Attending junior high and high school in the 1970s was great! Miniskirts and mini-dresses were popular and bellbottom pants became a huge success! Motown expanded into the 1970s and then came Disco. Not only did my generation set great clothing trends we also brought a new sound to music. (I think the youth of today may disagree.) Following the trend, I was fashionable, and with my perfectly shaped Afro I looked good!

The first time that I noticed Lance was in our first year at Ramona High School in Riverside, 1972. We attended different schools up until then. Back then high school started in the tenth grade. Only eighteen percent of the student body at Ramona was African American in the predominantly white school. Of all the black male students, one in particular stood out from the rest. Early on in my sophomore year I was walking down the hallway from one class to the next and I saw Lance coming towards me. From first glance I could tell that he was different from all the other Southern California boys. Lance was cool and he had a smooth slow walk. He wore a dark green turtleneck sweater, similar colored double knit slacks, shiny black shoes and a green apple hat cocked to the right side of his head. Everything about his demeanor impressed me. When our paths crossed Lance was smiling, popping his fingers and singing, with a beautiful voice, to a Motown hit. I was impressed at how well he could sing!

I thought, "Not bad!"

When Lance walked by me I complimented him, "Wow! You sing good."

He was smooth, "Oh, yeah?"

"Yes, you do," I flashed a smile.

Lance was very cool! He had a unique style about him unlike any that I had seen. I was attracted to more than just his outer appearance; Lance's inner warmth captivated me. Through his beautiful light golden brown and radiant eyes, I could see his kind soul. I just knew that he was a nice guy. At that time, I was not interested in dating Lance because I had a boyfriend, another sophomore (Clark), but I sure did like his style! Somehow I knew the day would come when our lives would intermingle in one way or another. I just didn't know at the time how deeply they would intertwine.

Soon after our first encounter Lance and I started hanging-out with the same circle of friends from school. In a group setting we frequented the local bowling alley, movie theaters, concerts, and house parties. To my surprise, two months after befriending Lance and while still dating Clark, I had a sexual dream about him. The content is not appropriate for me to divulge in this book, but I will share that the dream portrayed us as more than "just friends." When I awoke in my bed the steamy dream was still fresh in my mind.

"Wow! Where did that come from?" I thought.

"Oh, I don't think so!" I said aloud as the passionate moments played over and over again in my memory.

I wondered if my attraction to Lance was just physical. By this time, I knew that I liked him a lot. My initial impression of Lance as being a "nice guy" was correct! But there was more about him that piqued my interest, he was kindhearted, fun, outgoing, and of course very cool. I regularly flirted with him. Lance was a flirt too, and not just with me. I wondered how he would react to knowing that I had a dream about him. So, the next time that Lance and I were alone together I mentioned my dream to him. On school grounds during a lunch period, I had a few minutes to talk with Lance. We stood face-to-face flirting back and forth the whole time. When the moment was right I sprung it on him.

In my cutest voice, "I had a dream about you." (Pause)

Lance, seemingly unmoved, "Well, what was the dream about?"

I wanted to tell him but was hesitant because I knew that once I did it would take our relationship to a new level. Based on our flirtatiousness up to that point I am sure he sensed that my dream was one he wanted to hear more about, but being a "smooth" guy Lance played it down, "Tell me." Passionate memories of that dream reverberated over and over again in my mind bringing about the lustful desires that I had for him. I wanted Lance to know, but what I said was "I'm not going to say." Lance, with a sly smile on his face said, "then I know what it was about"! I knew his confidence of having me for more than a friend grew at that moment.

I continued dating Clark and befriending Lance the remainder of our sophomore year and throughout the summer break. Every time that Lance and I wound up at the same place among our friends we had fun together. We were able to converse about all sorts of things, including my relationship with Clark. Communicating back and forth with Lance became effortless. We found ourselves in each other's presence a lot, not just in person but by way of telephone, too. As our friendship grew we became more and more comfortable spending time together. The ease of how we related to one another did not escape either of us. Yet, we remained nothing more than close friends.

When I first met Clark, in the beginning of tenth grade, he was not as popular as he would become. After we started dating he tried out for the football team and as a sophomore made first string. He then started lifting weights. By the time our junior year came he had a beautiful body. Clark looked good! Once he realized that his new "muscular physique" caught the eye of many girls (including cheerleaders) his whole manner of dress and style changed. Clark developed a huge ego! Because of all the attention that he received he decided he didn't want to be restricted to dating just "one girl." Just weeks into our junior year he told me that he wanted to be free to date other people, which I didn't take kindly to. I thought that I was "all that and a bag of chips" and no way was I going to share my boyfriend with anyone else. Full of pride I said, "You can go and date other girls if you want to but you won't be dating me at the same time." He weighed his options but decided to date other girls anyway. Clark's yearning to explore his new-found popularity was overwhelming and we broke up. It was not long after our split that he wanted to come back but my ego would not let that happen. I said, "No!" He had made a mistake, one he later regretted, and I was not willing to take him back.

The following month Lance and I showed up, separately, to a gathering over at a mutual friend's house. A card game called "Bid Whist" (similar to Spades), which requires a partner, ensued. The prior year Lance had taught me how to play. He always wanted to partner with me. During the game I glanced over at Lance from across the table and without any warning whatsoever "ZING" just like that Cupid shot his arrow. Immediately a bell went off in my head "DING" and I thought, "No way!" Just then I realized my friendship for him had evolved into an undeniable love." Wow! What a revelation. It was weird because he had become a confidant and my buddy. Never, in a thousand years, did I think that my feelings for Lance would develop into love. But the truth was I cared deeply for him. Clark and I had broken up a couple of months before and I was enjoying an "uncomplicated" life of not having a boyfriend. I kept my feelings about Lance from him. My friend, Valerie, was the only one that I shared the information with. Lance and I continued a platonic relationship. We saw each other only in a group with other friends and that was just fine with me.

The Black Student Union, of which I was a member, put on a high school junior dance two weeks before Christmas at the University of California, Riverside. Lance and I attended separately. Not long after arriving I settled in and looked around to see who was there. I spotted Lance. At that very moment a song by "Marvin Gay (Let's Get It On) started booming over the sound system. I thought, "Man, I want to dance with him, really bad." Right then I saw Lance ask my friend (Valerie) to dance but she said, "No." She knew how I felt about him. Valerie decided to share with Lance that I liked him. She also said to him that he should ask me to dance. It was unlike Lance to step out of his "cool" and "slow swagger" stride but he did by making a quick dash over to me. I never saw him move that fast before. Lance and I still had time to dance before the Marvin Gay song ended. Let me tell you! "Let's Get It On" is one of the smoothest and most sensual "lustful songs" ever made. We leaned into each other in a slow grind. The feelings that rose up in me created a vivid memory of the sexy dream that I previously had about Lance. I lost all perception of time as I melted into his arms. It was one of those moments that I hoped would never end. After the night wound down Lance walked me to my car and our first kiss happened. It was all that I expected it to be and more. Although my body wanted more I knew that we should wait. So, the night ended with that one special kiss.

Ever since Cupid shot his arrow I wanted to date Lance but I was still enjoying being "unattached." After our first kiss I knew that the best was yet to come! The times that Lance and I spent together amongst our friends increased. We spoke more often on the phone and for much longer periods of time. I knew once

Lance and I started dating our friendship would quickly advance to sex and I wanted to keep it the way it was for a while longer.

The winter months went by fast and another summer break was coming quickly. In early June I showed up at a friend's house party. Lance was there, too. Soon after I arrived a Bid Whist game was about to start. Lance and I had become quite comfortable playing this game as partners. So, it was an obvious choice for him to seek me out. I never was a "drinker" nor did I ever like the taste of alcohol but because everyone else at the party was drinking I did, too. I was petite and the smallest amount of alcohol would get me tipsy. Someone from the party purchased cheap booze called "Brass Monkey." I drank too much and got drunk. When it was time to go home, Lance (like a gentleman), took me home and put me to bed, my parents were working at the restaurant at the time. While in bed I tried to kiss him but he would not reciprocate. In my drunken state, "Why not?" Lance while laughing, "Because you're drunk."

The following morning, I awoke with remembrances of the drunken events. Thoughts of my uncharacteristic behavior brightened when recalling how thoughtful Lance was towards me. He made sure that I was protected and well taken care of. I called Lance to let him know how much I appreciated him not taking advantage of me. His reply was simple, "I don't want you like that." What a huge impact that made on me! Lance had a chance to fulfill his sexual desires for me but didn't. Wow! He scored big points for that. My level of love for him rose even higher. Extra kudos!

Lance and I started spending copious amounts of time together, just the two of us. When our junior year ended we looked forward to road trips to the coast and just cruising around town. The both of us got our first cars just a couple of months before summer. My dad put a deposit down and I made the monthly payments on a brand new 1973 silver Mercury Capri. Lance's Aunt Val and Uncle Bennie gave him their 1972 Plymouth Satellite. Like most men, Lance drove everywhere. That car was his new "favorite toy." It did not take long for the novelty of having my first car to wear off, but not Lance, he spent more time driving than anyone that I knew. Many times he drove me to and from work.

A few weeks into our summer break Lance and I cruised around in his car. In his smooth laid back style he put his arm around me and said, "You want to be my girl?"

"Yeah" I said with a smile. That was it, we were officially a couple! As our relationship grew so did our passion for each other. We both wanted to experience sex together, and neither of us were virgins. We planned a day to unleash all of our intimate desires. I never knew that sex could be that good! It confirmed in my heart and mind that I wanted to be with Lance forever. I loved him! We became "High School Sweethearts." For all who are reading and romanticizing our relationship, please don't. I wish I had waited for marriage to enjoy the wonderful gift of sex!

Chapter 4

Marriage

(Lance)

Life was good! Robin and I saw a lot of each other during our last year of high school. Both of us were ahead of the required classes to graduate. We only had to attend school half days. Our senior year was a breeze! By one o'clock we were free to go wherever we wanted to. Robin and I both had part time jobs. She wanted independence from her parents and decided to no longer work at their restaurant. Sears hired Robin as a "Candy Girl." I worked as a short order cook at a steak and seafood restaurant. After school, when neither of us had to work, we hung out at Robin's house. Mr. and Mrs. Mitchell worked long hours at "Highland Haven BBQ", and it was not unusual for them to arrive home between one and two in the morning after being there from late morning. Kenny, was active in "Up with People" a diverse singing group that traveled at the time and Wayne and Craig kept busy with school and activities. So, that left Robin and me alone in her home a lot!

Because her parents were at work during the evenings we often used that time to be together. I made sure that I left in plenty of time before Mr. and Mrs. Mitchell came home, but not on one particular Saturday. That night Robin and I mistakenly fell asleep naked in her bed. We were awakened by the sound of her father's car entering the driveway and headlights shining through the bedroom window. Her parents were very cool but at the same time "old fashioned," especially when it came to their daughter having sex. Needless to say it would not have been good if they knew that we had been sleeping together.

In a matter of seconds Mr. Mitchell parked the car. Mrs. Mitchell was the first to make it to the front door and quickly, too. The first thing that Robin's parents always did when they got home late from work was to knock on her bedroom door to check in on her. We had about one minute to figure out what to do! Fear raced through our minds. I reached for my pants. Robin panicked, "Don't worry about getting dressed just get in the closet. "Hurry!" I ran "butt naked" into the closet but the door was slightly warped and it did not close all the way. There was a two-inch gap between the door and the doorframe. I knew that with enough light in the room her parents would be able to see me (nervously shaking) covering my private parts. Time seemed to pass in slow motion and there was an eerie quiet in the bedroom. Mr. Mitchell carried a revolver (snub nose 38) in a holster under his jacket wherever he went. The thought that if he caught me hiding in the closet he would take out his gun to shoot me did not escape my mind. Robin was able to shove my clothes under the bed and pull covers up to her neck right before her parents knocked on the door and then opened it. I was never so scared in my life! I just knew that I was going to get caught. If Robin's parents believed that she was sleeping and then quickly left the room, I thought, then I had a chance... but that did not happen. The last thing that I wanted was for her parents to stay and talk but that was exactly what they did. From the crack in the door I watched Mr. Mitchell turn the light on and ask Robin if she was awake. Robin carried on a conversation with her parents. I thought, "This can't be happening!" Mrs. Mitchell did not stay long but Mr. Mitchell sure did. He asked Robin about her day and shared how things went at the restaurant, too. I was beside myself! The longer their conversation went on the more convinced I was that I would be caught. After a few minutes of talking, which seemed like an eternity, her dad said, "Good night sweetheart." He then turned out the light and closed the door.

"Whew!" I thought, "That was a close one." When her father's footsteps got far enough down the hallway Robin said to me, "All clear." We quickly got dressed, but I could not find my socks and shoes. Robin in a frantic state of mind, "Don't worry about your shoes. Just go! You can get them later. I'll call Debbie to take you home. "Hurry!" When we were certain that her parents were in their bedroom I quickly and quietly scurried out of the house bare-footed.

After Robin located my shoes she called her best friend (Debbie), who lived across the street, to come over. Robin told her dad that she and Debbie were going out for donuts and she asked him if he wanted any. He said, "Yes." The first thing that Debbie and Robin did was drive to the end of the street to get me. When the three of us returned back to Robin's house she said to her parents, "We ran into Lance at the donut shop." In less than an hour a whirlwind of events took me from narrowly escaping being caught naked in Robin's bedroom closet to sitting at her kitchen table eating donuts with Mr. and Mrs. Mitchell. Crazy! Robin, Debbie, and I secretly laughed. Her parents did not have a clue to what actually went on. Later that night when Robin drove me home she made it clear, "NO MORE FALLING ALSEEP IN MY BED!"

After graduating from high school Robin and I went to Riverside City College. She wanted an Associate's Degree in General Education (prerequisite classes) with thoughts of going to law school later on. I also took General Education classes with thoughts of additional studies in Fire Science to become a Fireman. After completing my second semester in school, I became frustrated because I was just spinning my wheels. I wanted more out of life at twenty years of age than attending school and working a low paying (part-time) job as a cook. The thought of having to finish four years of college before making a decent paycheck bothered me. I wanted money in my pocket right then. I sat down with my Uncle Eddie to talk about future goals. He had enlisted in the Army right after high school. My uncle said, "As a young man, the Army would be a good starting point for your life. Maybe you can learn a trade while in the military which would help you for years to come?" After giving it a lot of consideration I joined the Army in February of 1977.

Robin and I agreed that the military would be a good thing for me. Although we didn't talk about marriage we did discuss having a life together after I got out of boot camp. We hoped that the Army would station me close to home. Robin and I were never apart from each other for a long periods of time, so we didn't know how things were going to go between us. She drove to Los Angeles to see me off at the airport. It was hard saying, "Goodbye."

I did not know how much I loved Robin until I arrived at boot camp in Fort Dix, New Jersey. I thought about her every day! We wrote back and forth. I was so excited to receive her letters. We talked on the phone when we could. I missed everything about Robin, her wit, charm, fun personality, amazing smile, beauty, engaging conversations, and of course her kisses. She was my best friend!

Getting through boot camp had its difficult moments but despite all the orders that were hollered at me, getting through the challenging obstacle courses and the grueling early morning (full gear) runs, none of that compared to the pain that I felt after reading a letter from a friend. A month into boot camp Kenny, a close friend from my high school, sent me a letter. He wrote, "I thought that you should know Robin has been seeing a basketball player from Riverside City College." In an instant my heart sunk to the pit of my stomach. I had to contact her right away to find out if it was true. In order to call Robin, I needed to sneak out of the barracks and hope that I did not get caught. I thought, "Any punishment that I could receive for calling Robin (on unscheduled time) would be worth it." I had to hear it straight from her. The night after receiving the letter I snuck out of the barracks and called Robin.

With my heart in pieces, "What's going on with this basketball dude? You're my girl!" Her reply was simple, "We are not married. Besides, it's nothing serious. We're just talking." Tears welled up in my eyes, "You broke my heart." Our conversation ended quickly. I was glad that I called to express my love for her but that did not stop the pain. To make matters worse I did get caught that night and I was put on KP Duty.

In WWII a "Jody" was used to describe a particular type of man. It is a generalized term meaning: any man that stays home while other men go to war. A "Jody" is often referred to as a man that gets to enjoy what the military men are missing, especially their girlfriends back home. While I marched in formation with the men from my squadron a sergeant led us in a cadence, "Ain't no sense in going home Jody's got your girl and gone. Sound off one, two, three, four. Ain't no use in looking down ain't no discharge on the ground." After the heartbreaking news about Robin and "the basketball dude" those words were hard to take. All I could think about was Robin... and someone else with "MY GIRL!"

After a few days of heartache, I had enough of the pain. I called Robin to get her back! With full confidence I said, "You're 'my' girl, and I want to marry you."

In the sweetest voice she said, "Really?"

The pain in my heart lessened, "Yeah, I really do."

She got excited, "Well, I want to marry you too but first you have to ask my father."

I did not understand, "I'm not marrying your father. I want to marry you."

Robin stood firm, "You have to get my daddy's approval."

I conceded, "Fine."

Mr. Mitchell was very busy running his restaurant so Robin set up a time for the two of us to talk by phone. I dated Robin for three years and in that time I got to know Mr. Mitchell well. Not only that but I had grown to respect him. Robin and I had spent many fun times with her parents. My freshman year of college, the four of us played together in a bowling league. Our team was called "The Pace Setters" and we won the league championship that year. Because of my close relationship with Mr. Mitchell I was comfortable asking for his daughter's hand in marriage. To my surprise, after asking him, he did not say yes right away.

Mr. Mitchell first asked me a couple of stern questions, "How are you going to support my daughter?" and "What are your plans for the future?"

My reply, "I plan on making a military career. Similar to what you did, sir. Robin is planning on getting a law degree. We will look for schools in Texas where I am stationed." My answers pleased him and I finally got his blessing to marry Robin!

I thought, "Now that I got permission to marry my sweetheart how do we go about planning a wedding? I will not get enough leave time from the Army to get married in California." At a young age I was taught that whenever I was uncertain about anything to pray about it. So I did, "God please make a way for us to get married right after AIT (Advanced Individual Training)." After graduation from boot camp, which Robin attended, I was allowed to go home for four days before flying to Virginia for training to become a tank mechanic (AIT). Having been away from Robin for six weeks during boot camp it was wonderful to see her again! Robin's soft kisses melted my lips.

Robin and her mother started planning the wedding. Debbie and Valerie helped pick out a wedding gown. We set the second of July as our date to get married, not knowing where I would be stationed after finishing two months of AIT. I was certain that the Army would give me a week or two of leave time (late June) after my training in Virginia ended. Many soldiers that entered the Army when I did were sent oversees soon after AIT but thankfully not me. God heard my prayers and because of that I received orders to be stationed stateside. Being sent anywhere in the USA was an answer to my prayer but God did one better than that. My orders were to a "Hometown Recruiters Office" in Riverside, California! God sure answered my prayer. Only one in about sixty thousand get sent back home to work in a recruiter's office. My orders were on a temporary (thirty day) basis. That was fine with me because it gave me plenty of time to get married and also spend some precious moments with my lovely bride.

I left Virginia and arrived in Riverside ten days before our wedding day. Right about that time Robin got strep throat. Thank God after seeing her doctor and taking prescribed penicillin she healed in time. Robin's father paid for the entire wedding. It took place in a chapel on March Air Force Base. Over two hundred attended. My entire family was there from Detroit, Ohio, Los Angeles, and New York, which made up close to half of the guests. They planned a family reunion for that week. The weather in sunny Southern California was perfect.

We had a full wedding party of ten all together. I asked my brother Michael to be the Best Man. Robin's brother Wayne, my Cousin Victor, and a close friend of mine (Ronnie), were also in the wedding party. Robin chose her close friend Debbie to be the Maid of Honor; the bridesmaids were Robin's friends Joyce, Heidi, and Valerie. I stood at the chapel's alter waiting for Robin to walk down the aisle on her father's arm. In her flowing white gown, she was a vision of beauty like a radiant angel.

When the time came to say our personal vows I was supposed to go first but I froze. I could not remember one word that I had memorized. The chapel was quiet; everyone was waiting for me to speak. Drawing a blank on what to say I became very nervous. My right leg shook uncontrollably and perspiration started forming around my neck. "Oh no" was the only thing that came to mind. After a very long pause I beckoned Robin with my eyes (more than once) to go ahead with her vows but she didn't. So, instead of a thoughtful and heartfelt declaration of my love for her I just said, "I love you." That was it. Nothing else entered my mind. Robin took that as a cue that I was done. It became very comical. She then completed her vows to me. During the wedding ceremony a woman with a beautiful voice sang our wedding song "Evergreen" by Barbara Streisand. She also sang a wonderful rendition of "Inseparable" by Natalie Cole.

There were endearing moments during the wedding reception. Robin and I first danced to "Let's Get It On" by Marvin Gaye, just like at our high school junior dance. This time our slow dance was not sensual, but full of love and anticipation for our life together. It was romantic. The father/daughter dance was very special. Robin cried on her father's shoulder throughout the entire song. I was so proud to lead my mother to the dance floor. During our song together she said that she was happy for me. I was the first in my family to get married and Robin the first in hers.

I only had a four-day weekend of leave time for my wedding and honeymoon combined. A friend of ours blessed us with a suite at a fancy hotel in Los Angeles for our wedding night. While in our suite Robin and I wanted to toast our marriage. Up until that point in my life I had never opened a champagne (cork) bottle before. I acted as if I knew how to open it but I really didn't. Robin stood by my side with anticipation as I somehow managed to get the cork partially out of the bottle using only my fingers, then proceeded to twist it with all my might until it "popped" off. The cork whizzed past her face missing by mere inches. I quickly apologized. Robin jokingly said, "Close call, are you trying to take me out already?" We had a good laugh then filled our champagne glasses. That was the happiest day of my life!

Chapter Five

Our First Home

(Lance)

For the short time that I was stationed in Riverside it did not make sense for Robin and I to get a place of our own. So, until the Army gave me orders elsewhere I moved in with Robin at her parents' house. It was great! Mr. and Mrs. Mitchell always treated me like family.

To my pleasant surprise the Army gave me two (thirty day) extensions to continue working at the Riverside recruiters office. What a blessing that was! It sure was nice staying in our hometown for the first few months of marriage.

I received orders to move to Fort Hood, Texas, by late September. After arriving in town Robin and I stayed in a motel for the first night. Robin awoke in the middle of the night sobbing, which woke me up. She was scared. I had no idea what was upsetting her.

I asked, "What's wrong?"

Her voice squeaked, "We don't know what we are doing. We don't know how we are going to make it. You lived with your aunt and uncle and I always lived with my parents. I'm afraid. What are we going to do? Do you know?"

I chuckled, "Yeah, I know. We're going to live, baby. That's what we're going to do."

She was uncertain, "What do you mean?"

With confidence in my voice, "We're all right. We've always been all right. You know?" The Carpenters song, "We've Only Just Begun" came to mind, and I began to sing to her. Robin snuggled along side of me as the song trailed off and we both fell back asleep.

Early the next morning I went to the financial office on base to collect a paycheck. The Army owed me three thousand six hundred dollars for back pay. That was a lot of money in the 1970s. At least it was to us. Up to that point in our lives neither of us had ever handled that much money at one time. They paid me in cash! I was grinning from ear-to ear upon walking back into our motel room. Robin was too after seeing me flash the cash. Spontaneously I tossed the money onto the bed. With elation we threw it up into the air over and over again, laughing and singing, "We're in the money. We're in the money."

After our celebration I went to work and Robin went apartment hunting. By the time that I got home that night we had a place to call home! Robin went shopping for furniture, appliances, dishes, linens, etc. She decorated every room beautifully. Robin touched my heart by taking pride in our first home together. That was a wonderful time in our marriage. We bonded more than ever before.

We quickly got into marriage routines. With only one car between us (I had given mine to my cousin), Robin would drop me off at work then go about doing her daily errands. It was of God that the Army stationed me in Texas because we lived away from our families, which forced us to rely solely on each other.

Robin and I regularly went shopping together at the BX (on base discount store). On one particular day we came across a very nice component set for $260. I said to Robin, "My Motown record collection would sure sound good on this component."

She quickly replied, "Let's buy it!" I wanted it too, but money was tight. "Well, we really cannot afford it right now, but we can save up for it. In about two months we'll be able to get it." She understood, "Ok."

Not long afterwards, Robin's parents came for a visit while I was at work. When I arrived home Robin was there, Mr. and Mrs. Mitchell were staying in a motel nearby. To my surprise the stereo component set that I liked was set up in our living room. I asked Robin, "Where did this come from?"

"My daddy bought it for me." I was furious!

"Well, you need to take it back."

"No, I'm not going to take it back. My daddy bought it for me."

"You need to take it back, Robin!"

"I'm not taking it back."

"Yes you are. You are going to take it back!"

"I'm not taking anything back, my daddy bought it for me."

"Take it back!"

"You must be out of your mind. I'm not taking it back!"

She didn't understand why I was mad. I wanted to do something special by saving up the money to buy it for her. That was our first married fight, which she won, the component stayed. Later she apologized for not understanding and promised not to do that again.

Some of the best years of our lives were in Fort Hood. We quickly made friendships with other married couples from the Army base, James (aka Smoky) and Janice, Roscoe and Marilyn. Jeff Smith befriended us, too, just to name a few. Some of them we still keep in touch with today. We got together for weekly socials with our friends at our apartment or their homes. It was so much fun carrying-on, laughing and playing games with them. Robin started work as a grade school substitute teacher. She received an acceptance letter from a pre-law school in Austin, which was about thirty-five miles away. Life was good!

There was a bingo night on base every month. Occasionally Robin went with her girlfriends. She was always good and lucky at playing games. Robin won at almost everything. She only went to bingo night when we were low on money. I had no doubt that she would come home with some cash. It was only a matter of time before she would yell out, "BINGO!" One night she won five hundred dollars. "That's my girl!"

I found ways to bring in some extra cash, too. My Detroit roots stayed with me. The "Little Hustler" will always be a part of who I am. Many of the Army guys would party a lot especially on the weekends. They got paid on a Friday and by the time Monday rolled around they were hurting for money. That pattern occurred all the time. They were so desperate for cash after blowing all their money on girls and booze that they agreed to pay me back dollar for dollar on loans. Shoot, I would be a fool not to take that kind of return on my money. I did not go out with the guys after work and throw away money. I enjoyed a "home-life" with my wife.

To my surprise, after nine months in Fort Hood, I received orders to go to Germany for six months. My contract stated that I would stay stateside for at least the first twenty-eight months after boot camp. That was part of the Army recruiter's sales pitch to get me to sign up. I was mad and marched right down to the Adjutant General's Office (Human Resources) to show them my contract and state my case!

Officer, "Yeah, it says that but we can send you anywhere that we want to on a temporary basis at any time."

I was taken back, "Excuse me?"

Officer, "Technically you will still be stationed in Fort Hood."

I thought, "Technically my body is going over to Europe and no part of me is going to be in Fort Hood."

I replied furiously, "This contract is pretty ambiguous. The contract isn't even worth the paper it's written on! You told me that I would be stationed stateside for twenty-eight months. I come here and set up a home with my wife, she enrolled in college and now you are about to send me away?"

Officer, "Yeah, that's just the way it is."

I continued to fight for my rights but in the end, I lost and had to go. The last thing that the officer said to me before I walked out, "Either go to Germany or to the stockade, it's your choice."

I couldn't see any sense in Robin staying in our apartment for six months while I was overseas. So, January 1978, we packed up our belongings and put most of it in storage. She put law school on hold. Robin did not want to drive back to California by herself and I didn't have any leave time, so her brother (Wayne) flew to Texas and drove back to Riverside with her. Robin was happy to be able to spend time at her parent's home while I was away.

We talked on the phone when we could. Robin wrote me letters almost every day and sent care packages, too. I looked forward to receiving them. It was a big deal to open the boxes and see what was inside! The Army provided for my housing and food while I was in Germany. Robin stayed at her parents' home rent-free. That made it easy for us to save money during that time. I sent my checks home to our credit union. I lived off my earnings from poker games and my lending business. After four months of being apart I had amassed a few thousand dollars. Since I had leave time and some extra money, I decided to buy a plane ticket for Robin to come to Germany. We spent two wonderful weeks together.

Before flying out of California Robin bought both of us a pair of 1970s style (unisex) blue jeans. Each pant leg had many zippers. She didn't know that while I was in Germany I had been regularly working-out. I was in the best shape of my life! The jeans that she bought for me were for the waist size that I was before I went overseas. When I put on the jeans they were way too big for my waist. Robin was petite, for fun she wanted me to try on her unisex jeans and to our surprise they fit. We had a good laugh!

Robin and I enjoyed time together sightseeing. It was springtime, the grass was green, flowers were blooming and birds singing. We drove to a small, quaint, mountainous town in Germany, Garmisch-Partenkirchen. Its restaurants served more than just good German food. We experienced many other types of cultural cuisine, including French, Italian, Polish, and Spanish. It was some of the best foods in the world! Also, while in Germany, we visited Neuschwanstein Castle. The magnificent fortress inspired Walt Disney to create "Magic Kingdom." It was spectacular! After exploring most of Germany we decided to cross the Austrian border. Austria was beautiful! Especially the enormous Alps, they were stunning and breathtaking all at the same time.

After a great vacation it was hard saying goodbye. I did not want Robin to leave. We continued speaking on the phone and writing back and forth. A few weeks went by and I received a phone call from Robin. She started the conversation with, "Guess what?" I didn't know, "Not a clue. What?"

She sprang it on me, "I'm pregnant."

I was thrilled! Robin knew that I wanted to start a family right after getting married but she wanted to wait until after finishing law school. Robin was on birth control pills but when I went overseas she didn't see the need in taking them anymore. When she came to visit me we used birth control (most of the time), I guess it was during one of those passionate times that I forgot!

To my pleasant surprise the Army sent me back to the states two weeks early. Robin drove back to Fort Hood in our car with her friend Debbie. They took turns driving. Robin said that the trip was comical because Debbie had never driven a vehicle with a stick shift before. Robin gave her a quick lesson then off they went. Crazy! Once back in Texas we got another apartment and enjoyed spending time with our friends again. Robin did not get a job this time around or start pre-law school. She wanted to raise our son as a stay-at-home-mom just like her mother did. April 16, 1979, God blessed us with a son, Karama. Robin and I were so excited. Life was good.

Towards the end of 1980 I had to make a decision to renew for another four years in the Army, as of February 1981, or get out. I did enjoy life in the military. The deciding factor, however, was that I couldn't trust the Army. Not after guaranteeing me to be stateside for two years then sending me to Germany.

I asked Robin if she wanted to stay in Texas and she said, "No, I want to go home." The both of us agreed that going back to California would be best. Although we met many wonderful people and made close friendships in Fort Hood, Texas, we belonged in Riverside. Besides, Robin wanted to be there for her mother. She was diagnosed with breast cancer only months before. So, the day after my discharge papers were handed to me we loaded up a U-Haul, attached it to our car, and headed back West!

Chapter Six

Marital Trouble

(Robin)

Lance, Karama (eighteen months old), and I temporarily moved into my parents' house. Finding work was our first priority. Due to my mother's illness my father decided to sell the restaurant. At this time, he also was looking for employment. Lance quickly got hired as the director of a Hunt Park community recreational center program. I entered into Thrifty's management training program. Thrifty's is now known as Rite Aid. My father landed a union job assembling airplanes at Rohr Aircraft and quickly worked his way up to chief shop steward.

Lance did not like his new line of work very much. For one thing his salary was a lot less than what he earned while in the Army and secondly overseeing recreational programs did not interest him. He quit after only seven weeks on the job. Lance looked for employment elsewhere that would better suit him. The next job that he took was in a factory assembling various tanks for scuba divers and astronauts. Lance caught on very fast and because of that he thought the job was a good fit but that was not the case. He disliked the physical aspect of his position. Lance said he did not want to work manual labor for the rest of his life. So he quit that job, too. My mother advised him, "Do not quit a job before having another one lined up." My mom always gave wise, prudent advice, but Lance didn't take it.

Lance was dealing with the same (career choice) issues that he had before joining the Army. After much thought (January, 1981) he decided to return to Riverside City College using "educational benefits" that the Army provided. Because of his years in service the government paid him six hundred dollars per month while attending school.

While in school Lance searched for a part time job. His military experience helped him get employed as a security guard. Shortly after starting work he realized that he did not like that type of work either. After being employed for only a month he quit but remained in school.

Things were going well in our lives. Lance regularly took walks at night around our neighborhood. After coming home from one of those walks he shared with me that he came across some very nice tract-homes. He said that he prayed right then, "God I would like to own a home like these to raise my family in." I became excited about the possibility of owning a house!

By the spring of that same year Aunt Val called Lance and informed him that she had heard of law enforcement employment opportunities opening in our area. Lance eagerly looked into it right away! After studying for and taking the law enforcement test to join the Riverside Police Department, Lance thought he had passed but that was not the case. He then took the Department of Corrections test to become a correctional officer and passed! Because of Lance's years in the Army he received preference points. God opened up a door of opportunity for Lance that he had been waiting for. He finally had a long-term career. He no longer needed to attend college.

Because Lance had a secure job and I became an assistant manager at Thrifty's we were able to afford our own apartment again. Seven months after moving back to California the three of us moved out of my parents' house. We rented a two-bedroom apartment on Satinwood Street in Rialto. For the first time Karama had his own bedroom. All three of us were very happy!

I made friends at work pretty fast. I especially became close to another assistant manager, Wanda, and we became best friends. As we were talking one day we decided to plan a day trip on our day off. We planned to go to "The Price Is Right" game show. Hollywood was only a short drive away. One of our coworkers (John) went, too. I just knew that I could win if given a chance to play. Like Lance said, I was always lucky. Now I call it "godly favor". When I was sixteen years old and without any beauty pageant experience, I won the Miss Black Teenage San Bernardino Pageant. I was also the first African American girl in the history of my high school to be voted Homecoming Queen. I always believed I could achieve anything that I put my mind to.

I was excited to go to a game show for the first time. Before leaving my home for Hollywood I kissed Lance goodbye. He playfully teased me.

"You're not going to win."

"Yes I am."

"Nah, you're not going to win anything."

"Yes I am, you'll see."

During the drive John, Wanda and I discussed the possibility of getting selected from the audience. We knew the odds were not good for all three of us to get to play The Price Is Right, but we just hoped that at least one of our names would be called.

Once we arrived at the studio there was a long line of people ahead of us waiting to get in. A female representative from the show met briefly with everyone in line and asked us to share something about ourselves. When it was my turn I said matter-of-factly, "There really isn't all that much interesting to say. I have a son and I am married." Curiously I continued, "But you know what? If you have a car in there I could really use a convertible."

The representative stated, "I don't know if we have a convertible."

Candidly I replied, "I'll take a Volkswagen Bug. I don't care, I just need a car!"

She laughed and moved on down the line of possible contestants. I hoped that I had left an impression on her.

By the time that we got into the studio the only available seats were in the front row. I said to Wanda and John that I had never seen anyone "come down" from the front row. I was a little disappointed with where our seats were, but the atmosphere was charged with excitement and we were having fun. Normally on game shows the contestants jump up and down, scream and act really silly when they are chosen. I told my friends that if I did get called I definitely would not act like that. We all agreed we would be cool and calm.

Shortly into the beginning of The Price Is Right an announcer called the first contestant. A man's name was heard and sure enough he was from the back of the studio. Just as I said, this grown man jumped up and down and skipped down the aisle with his arms wildly flailing in the air. He acted real silly with excitement. Before the second contestant was called the studio got very quiet and then I heard the announcer yell out, "Robin Croom come on down!" I immediately burst into excitement by jumping up and down. Go figure. The shock of hearing my name overtook me. I guess it's impulsive to act silly on a game show when you have been selected to be a contestant. Oh well, so much for cool and calm!

Of the four podiums I stood second from the right. The first merchandise to bid on was fishing gear and I guessed the closest without going over! I then ran up the stairs and hugged Bob Barker. The fishing gear was mine to keep. The game that I played on stage consisted of guessing the actual prices on grocery items. I did not get enough of them correct and because of that no prize was given.

After two more contestants won their way onto the stage the three of us spun the "Big Wheel" for a chance to get into the Showcase round. Each of us had two spins to equal one dollar or come as close as we could. The contestant that spun the highest amount without going over one dollar moved on to the final round. The contestant that spun the wheel before me scored eighty-five cents. I thought, "That is going to be hard to beat."

My first spin landed on forty-five cents and my second fifty cents. I wound up winning! There were three more contestants playing the game so I had to wait until they made their way to the "Big Wheel." The winner of their spin joined me in the Showcase round.

Because the woman that I was competing against won her game on stage she had the choice of bidding on the first showcase or defer it to me. She deferred. Not only did I guess closer on my showcase than she did to hers, but I also guessed within $100 of the actual value and won both showcases! The showcases included a mink coat, bedroom set, water purification system, exercise equipment, trips to New Orleans, Rome, and Africa. But no car, not even a Volkswagen Bug!

The first thing that I said to Lance when arriving home, nonchalantly, "I won."

He wasn't convinced, "You didn't win anything."

With a big smile I whipped out my new mink coat, "Oh yes I did!"

The game show rules were that all three trips (Rome, Africa, and New Orleans) had to be taken within a consecutive three-week period. With our busy work schedules and Karama being so young we couldn't go away for that long of a time, so we discussed which one of the three trips that we would take. I wanted to go to Africa and Lance favored New Orleans because he said he had never been on a cruise. He soon found out that a riverboat down the Mississippi was NOT a cruise. Touring Africa seemed more exciting to me. We wound up going to New

Orleans, which turned out to be the worst vacation that we had ever been on. The riverboat was very old and not kept up well. The Mississippi was at low-tide and extremely muddy. To top it off I got strep throat and had to get off the boat and seek medical treatment. I am sure that the trip to Africa would have been much better. But on second thought, being out of the country with strep throat would have been horrible.

Lance was put on the night shift at his new job, which ended at eleven pm. I was in bed early because my work shift at Thrifty's started by seven in the morning. We were not spending that much time together, however the differences in work schedules did help with watching Karama. Lance woke up before I left the house. He then could spend the day with our son. By the time he had to go to work I was home. My parents helped, too. Since Karama was their first grandchild they looked forward to loving on him whenever they could.

Shortly into starting work at the prison Lance began hanging out with fellow correctional officers after work. It became a regular occurrence. Sometimes he didn't come home until two in the morning. He never called to say how late he would be. I wasn't concerned that he stayed out to the wee hours in the morning with the "guys;" I was annoyed that he didn't consider my feelings. I shouldn't have had to worry (not knowing) if he was all right. One phone call was all that I asked of him.

Besides the time when Lance was in Germany we always slept together. We expressed our feelings for each other through our intimate moments together. When Lance started working nights the intimacy in our marriage slowly faded away because when he got to bed I was either asleep or sleepy. We were sexually active but it became just sex. As if two people were going through the motions without a loving connection between them. We started growing apart. Everyday Lance went his separate way and I went mine. He became less and less interested in my thoughts and aspirations. I felt like he did not support me in any way. We used to have mutual interests but that went away, too. Instead, the distance between us widened each day. We used to talk about everything but by this time in our marriage we didn't talk about anything of significance. To make matters worse, neither of us offered any resolution to our marital problems. Our life together was becoming mundane and our once thriving relationship as best friends since high school was dying.

My emotional needs were not being met and Lance and I became more and more distant. That former flirtatious spirit revived itself and I became a huge flirt at work among my peers. As the devil would have it, I caught the eye of one of the other managers, a younger man, who was definitely attracted to me. One thing led to another and before I knew it we were having an affair. Since he was single, there were few obstacles and we were able to go to his house for our sexual encounters. The affair only lasted about six months before I brought it to an end. Lance was so busy doing his thing that he did not know.

Because there were many times that Lance did not come home right after work I thought that he might have been cheating on me, but I never questioned him on it. The affair that I had fulfilled a void that my husband once filled. I missed the tender moments that two young lovers share together. During the affair my emotions were all over the place. There were times when I felt that my actions were justified and other times I felt guilty for being dishonest and unfaithful. The temporary fulfillment always gave way to shame and pain.

Because Lance was making good money at the Correction Department and I earned a decent salary as an assistant manager we could afford to buy nice things, including a house. God answered Lance's prior prayer. In the spring of 1982 we bought a brand new tract-home in Rialto (twenty miles from Riverside). We were beyond excited!

The spacious three-bedroom two-bath (single story) home had a full sized dining room, sunken living room, den with a fireplace, which was conveniently located off the kitchen. It was perfect for entertaining guests. The builder let me pick out a (beige) carpet ahead of time. Because the house was at the end of a cul-de-sac it came with an extra-large front and back yard. We negotiated into the sale price landscaping and a back patio with lattice covering. To top it off the house came with a three-car garage. We were blessed!

I looked forward to decorating Karama's bedroom. At three years of age he was "all boy." He loved throwing a ball around so I chose a sports theme with matching bedspread and curtains. Lance and I wanted to plan our next baby, unlike Karama who came as a surprise. Although we were not ready for another child yet, I painted a baby's room ahead of time in neutral (yellow and white) colors.

Lance and I hosted many socials in our new home the first being a housewarming party. Friends and family members blessed us with lots of nice things. We enjoyed hosting so much that we looked forward to entertaining guests for any occasion. I recall one particular Halloween party my "dapper dad" showed up at our house wearing a diaper, bib and sucking on a pacifier. It was hilarious!

Lance and I spent a lot of money decorating our house. It was fun getting it to look just the way we wanted. At least once a year we took a family vacation. Karama did not lack for anything, we provided for all his needs. Money went towards our personal interests, too. We thought that we were living the American dream.

Over the next year our lives stayed on the same course. Since our work hours continued to be so different, we had little time together to concentrate on our problems and the distance between us continued to grow each passing month. It was something that we both felt but neither of us wanted to talk about. We looked forward to throwing the next house party because it brought us together even if it was just for one night. Our marriage was in the danger zone, but neither one of us acknowledged it. All the material possessions and worldly fun that we were having masked the impending precipice that we were about to fall over.

Chapter Seven

Brink of Divorce

(Robin)

The "good life" that we seemed to be living did not last all that long. The partying at our home increased to the point where Lance was regularly having poker nights with his friends. He was introduced to cocaine and started using it only on occasional weekends. He convinced me to indulge as well. Even though I enjoyed the high that the drug gave, I didn't want to spend my hard earned money on it. Once I realized that Lance had an addiction problem with cocaine and started craving it more frequently, I refused to participate. I didn't want to be a party to anything that would eventually harm my husband. Well, that separated us even further. Throwing house parties and getting high were the last two links that we had between us besides our son. Lance found others to get high with. Lance got to the point that he would use our mortgage money and sell his jewelry to get his drug. Our finances were a mess and we were using our credit cards, which got us into debt.

Lance and I communicated less and less. We just went through the motions of marriage without much of a connection to each other. We settled into complacency. We were not the argumentative type but sometimes silence can be worse than a fight. In retrospect I understand what happened to us. Our minds were focused on the things of the world and we had temporarily lost our way. Satisfying our fleshly desires became our passion and we lost all control. We both needed an adjustment in our thinking, which would lead to a change in our behavior.

Work was an outlet for me. Of all of our regular customers at Thrifty's one in particular stood out from the rest. A woman in her early forties seemed to make it a point to locate me wherever I was in the store. When she found me she always wanted to talk about Jesus and how much He loved me. She often said that she would pray for me. I wasn't open to hear any of that at the time. In fact, I avoided this woman as much as possible. If I saw her walking in the front door I would quickly make my way to the back of the store. My escape attempts were futile. She seemed to be on a mission and no matter where I hid she found me.

In February 1983, on my way to work, I had an encounter with God. I will never forget it. I was twenty-six years old, and it was around the same time that the church lady from my job was harassing me. (At least that is how I looked at it at that time.) As I was driving, there was a bright (dawn) sunlight shining through my windshield. It was beautiful and peaceful at the same time. I sensed a tugging on my heart. Unsure of what I was experiencing, somehow I knew that it was God reaching out to me. Through the searing bright light of the sun I sensed that God was saying,

"Robin, it's time for you to turn your life around and let me into your heart." I had never experienced the presence of the

Holy Spirit before. I just knew, without a doubt, that God was entreating me to change my ways. I had no idea how to go about doing that, but I wanted to.

Two of Lance's aunts and uncles attended Loveland (Christian) Church. Lance and I had not been attending any church. Early autumn of that same year his Aunt Sonia asked me if I wanted to attend "The God's Woman Conference." I felt convicted of my sins instantly and knew that I needed to make some changes in my life. I accepted the invitation. The conference took place fifty-five miles north of Riverside in Palm Springs.

During the conference the atmosphere was filled with the presence of God and He pierced my heart. I didn't know what to do with all the feelings that were overpowering my senses. As if there were only two people in a conference room filled with women, God placed my gaze on a powerful woman of God nicknamed "Mom" Brewington. I was led to approach her and ask if I could talk to her. She agreed to come to my room after the session. I was nervous and not sure what I would say to her. When she walked into my room all the emotions inside of me came out through the tear ducts in my eyes. She instantly put her arms around me and asked why I was crying. I told her about everything that was going on in my life and to my relief she didn't judge me. She held me tighter and told me how much God loves me and that He wanted to forgive me of my sins. I had heard that before, but on this night I accepted it. It was that night in the comfort of a hotel room that I gave my life to Jesus Christ! I felt "brand new" and I knew my life would never be the same. As I drove home from the conference I knew that my sins were forgiven and that I was a new creation through the sacrificial blood of Jesus Christ. I couldn't wait to get home and share with Lance the transformation that had taken place within me! I thought the same excitement would fill his heart too. After arriving home those hopes were dashed. After sharing everything that had taken place at the conference and the awesome experience that I had with the Lord, I told Lance that we needed to find a church to go to and allow God to turn our lives around. To my dismay he didn't feel what I felt or see things the way I saw them. He said, "I'm not ready to go, but you can go if you want to."

Many years later I had the occasion to see the "church" lady at a marriage conference and was able to share with her the fruits of her labor. The seeds that she planted bloomed at the God's Woman Conference in the desert of Palm Springs!

After many attempts spanning over several weeks to convince Lance of why we should go to church as a family, he gave in. I wanted to go to church every Sunday but we only went occasionally. After a while the fire that I experienced in the desert started to die down and I found myself falling back into the "lukewarm" lifestyle that my husband was comfortable living. We were going to church, but one foot was still in the world. God would have his way with us but it was a process and we were going to go through some trials and challenges that would eventually bring us both to our knees!

In spite of the fact that our marriage was on "life support" we decided to have another child. Although it wasn't spoken, Lance and I thought having another child would bring us closer together, plus we didn't want too great of an age gap between our children. By November I got pregnant! As each passing month went by my longing to stay home and raise my children became a pressing desire in my heart. I thought about how I was raised. I remembered my mom always being there for us and I wanted to be like my mother. I got a taste of staying home with Karama after he was born but when Lance departed from the Army we both needed to find work.

June 1984, (seven months pregnant) I decided that I no longer wanted to work at Thrifty's because I wanted to be home (full time) to raise my children. Lance was not feeling that idea. After I shared my reasons for wanting to leave Thrifty's he said, "That was not part of the plan. We said that we would both work, buy a nice house, have two Mercedes in the garage and get ahead."

Not too long afterwards we went to church and the sermon was on the responsibility of a husband. A couple of days went by and while at home Lance shared with me that during the sermon he felt as if God spoke directly to him. He mentioned a couple of things that our Pastor said, "Man was made to be the chief bread winner and that women should be a helpmate." I understand that in many households both the husband and the wife have to work to support the family, but I also have to acknowledge that it is a difficult job to be mom, wife, and worker all at the same time. When Lance told me that after maternity leave I did not have to return to Thrifty's, I was thrilled!

I knew that our finances would be stretched tight so I started thinking about what I could do at home to bring some additional monies into the household. I understood how hard it was to find good childcare so when the thought to open a childcare business came into my mind, I felt it was a "no-brainer." Lance was on board with the idea and I did everything necessary to fulfill the requirements to open our home to receive other working moms' children. While loving on my two, I could love on a few more!

August 12, 1984, our second son (Kashif) was born. Lance and I were so happy! Kashif literally and figuratively brought new life back into our home. Lance and I were doing well and we were communicating more but soon things reverted back and the distance between us grew once again. As I look back, the mistake we made was not acknowledging the problems that were plaguing our marriage. We ignored all the warning signs in hope that it would all work out. We needed help, but we refused to acknowledge it, and then seek others for the help needed. A marriage just doesn't "fall apart," there are subtle "exits" that we make along the way. God can fix anything that we give to him!

My daycare business consisted of Kashif (an infant), two other babies from friends of mine, Karama (five years old), and two other children close to his age. Every day was the same, changing diapers, making meals, cuddling babies and tending to the children's every need. When the parents came to take their children home I still had to look after my own two boys. There was no break!

Every once in a while I was able to get away from the daily grind, like when Wayne and I decided (November, 1984) to go to Hollywood for a chance to be on the "Let's Make A Deal" show. We knew the odds of getting chosen to be contestants were slim, but that didn't stop us from going. To increase the possibility of both of us being selected we decided not to stand in line together.

The game show studio was filled with people dressed in all different kinds of costumes, each one hoping his or her appearance would catch the eye of the host, Monty Hall. Wayne and I knew that only a few would get chosen to play, so our outfits had to be eye-catching. Being that my brother was a bodybuilder he decided to come as a professional looking weightlifter. Wayne's bulging muscles helped him stand out from everyone else in the crowd. I wore a very cute cheerleader outfit with matching ribbons in my hair. Although I had two children by this time, I could pull this off because I remained in great shape.

Wayne sat in the middle of a row towards the front of the studio. I found a spot a few rows behind him, just two seats in from the isle. No one knew ahead of time who would be selected but when I watched the show on TV at least one person closest to the isle seemed to get picked. After Monty started the show by greeting the TV viewers and introducing himself he walked up and down the aisle looking for the first contestant. I tried to get his attention by looking the part of a high school cheerleader by being perky and using my cute (girlish) smile – and that worked! Remember, I am an experienced gamer now!

As Monty was about to walk by my row he spotted me then stopped. I got very excited!

He asked me, "What's your name?"

"Robin Croom," I replied with a beaming smile.

I stood up then spontaneously started jumping up and down.

Monty said, "I want to buy your purse for two hundred dollars."

He took cash out of his suit jacket pocket and counted off two hundred dollars. I picked up my purse and handed it to him in exchange for the money.

Monty jokingly said, "Wow! That's a heavy purse. You must have a lot of valuables in there."

"No," I said with an uncontrollable smile.

Monty, "Well I am going to empty it out anyway."

His assistant (Dean) came over with a large (clear) plastic bag. Monty handed me his microphone while he used both hands to empty the contents of my purse into the bag for everyone watching on TV to see. I was so embarrassed that I covered my face with my hands, nervously laughed, and said, "Oh man." When Monty finished he handed me the bag with all my personal belongings and said, "We don't want this, just your purse for two hundred dollars.

Monty handed the cash to me then turned away and took three steps down the aisle. I sat back down. Everything happened so fast. I didn't know what to make of it besides that I just gave my purse away for two hundred dollars. I was hoping for an opportunity to win a much larger prize. The crowd became excitingly loud when Monty walked away from me because they thought he was searching for another contestant.

"Hold it gang," Monty said jokingly to the crowd.

He stopped walking then turned to look at me.

Monty continued, "I'm still talking to Robin."

He remained a few feet away and asked me, "You have two hundred dollars – that could buy what we have in our display."

A curtain on stage opened up and a female model appeared standing next to a very tall box. I leaped to my feet and without hesitation said, "Yes!" Monty walked up to me and I handed him back the cash.

"Show Robin what's in the box," Monty instructed the model.

As the merchandise appeared Monty explained the "great deal" that I made in a stereotypical game show voice. Like when I was selected as a contestant on "The Price Is Right" show, "Robin Croom COME ON DOWN!"

Monty, "Robin, for your two hundred dollars you got a BRAND NEW WASHER AND DRYER and a STEAMER CARPET CLEANER!

The game show narrator spoke over the PA system explaining the make and model of the appliances, as well as the value, nine hundred sixty dollars. That was expensive back in the mid 1980s. The audience clapped along with me. I was thrilled!

Monty wasn't done with me yet. He said, "Now you have the washer, dryer, and steam cleaner."

Just then Dean walked down the aisle carrying a large red and white polka dot box. Monty took the top of the box off and to my surprise out came my purse with a crisp five-hundred-dollar bill hanging out of it.

Monty asked me, "You can keep the washer, dryer, and steam cleaner and the five hundred dollars or you can choose what's behind door number three?"

I took a deep breath and a long pause then made up my mind, "I'm keeping what I have."

Monty handed me the five-hundred-dollar bill and then said, "Well let's see what's behind the curtain."

A female model was standing next to a large cow as a booby prize. I was relieved that I made the right choice by not getting greedy. Monty smiled and handed me back my purse. He said, "I'm not keeping your purse. You can have it; we don't want it." That was a lot of fun! Wayne looked back at me and gave a huge smile.

After two more contestants were selected from the audience, (unfortunately Wayne wasn't one of them), and their deals were made, Monty asked the three of us to stand up. He asked each contestant if we wanted to trade in our prize for what was behind curtains one, two, and three. I and one other contestant said yes.

Monty shared that behind one of the curtains was merchandise worth eleven thousand fifty dollars. Wayne came over and stood next to me. I chose curtain number one and the other contestant chose number two.

Monty revealed curtain number three first, which neither of us would have won. Displayed were a brand new electric typewriter, telephone equipped with an answering machine, and a complete encyclopedia set. All three were very popular "back in the day." The combined value, one thousand six hundred dollars. The other contestant picked the grand prize curtain, a TV and stereo entertainment system, as well as a fur coat. My prize (Whirlpool kitchen appliances) was worth two thousand three hundred eighty-seven dollars, which was more than double the value of what I won earlier. That was a great experience!

I needed more fun times like that because my home-life wasn't going so well. My marriage was in trouble and after one year of running the daycare business, I began thinking of doing something different. I knew I would miss the babies that God put in my care, but it was hard enough taking care of my two around the clock, then add four more! When I informed the parents of my decision they were disappointed because I took great care of their children. I thought about other types of businesses that I could start. One day it occurred to me, "I love getting my nails done. I can do that for a living. I am a people person so I would do well as the owner of a nail salon." Money was tight and I needed to go to cosmetology school. So, my daddy paid for the schooling.

It was a very exciting time in my life because I was about to embark on a new business venture! At twenty-eight years of age the daycare business was behind me. I had just enough money to open a nail salon. By this time Karama was in kindergarten. When he got home from school Lance or my mother took care of him and Kashif, too.

I named my new business "Heavenly Nails" it was located in Bloomington, conveniently just a mile away from my home. Lance did not take any interest in my nail salon or even the daycare for that matter. His lack of involvement led us to drift even further apart. Day in and day out we just went through the motions of a typical family life without any real meaning behind it.

My business was located in a small (three unit) strip mall. While setting up the shop, a man named Rico just so happened to be setting up his new (men's apparel) store, which was right next-door. He was very friendly. Rico was six years older than me. He was married and had two children at a very young age from a previous marriage. They were grown and had moved out on their own by this time.

While preparing my shop for opening day, Rico offered to help me get (much needed) fixtures. I was hoping that Lance would help me with that but he showed zero interest in my business. So, I accepted Rico's help.

I was a flirt and Rico was a smooth talker. Two ingredients that are not good when you are suffering in a struggling marriage. We were headed (full steam ahead) to an affair. Everyday Rico made it a point to walk over to my shop. I started looking forward to it. The one-on-one attention that I desired from my husband instead started coming from Rico. Lance emotionally detached from me and Rico filled the void. After many days of flirting with Rico he made a sexual remark about my lips.

In my most sensual tone, "Do you want to kiss them?"

Eagerly he replied, "Yes!"

Rico was not the typical kind-of-guy that I had been attracted to. Especially knowing that less than two years' prior to our meeting he was released from prison, but he satisfied a desire of mine that my husband used to fill. Rico talked with me every day and seemed to genuinely care about my concerns. I shared with him things I used to talk to Lance about.

Well, after our first kiss it did not take long before Rico and I were having sex in either my shop or his. There were times when we went to a motel room, but as time progressed we took even bigger risks by having sex in our own homes when our spouses were away. I'm not proud of this time in my life, but I share it because I know that it may help someone else. I want to "keep it real" so another marriage may be saved from the hurt, pain and betrayal that are a bi-product of extramarital affairs. That includes not only physical affairs, but emotional affairs too! Don't be deceived!

My infatuation with Rico was not physical. It was his personality, not his outer appearance, that attracted me. He fulfilled a need that was missing in my marriage. Rico gave me much needed attention that I yearned for and he treated me well. I started to crave something that God forbade and I believed that it was okay, even though deep in my heart I knew I was going down a path that would bring much destruction!

Lance did not know anything about my relationship with Rico either, because he was still too busy doing "his thing." If he had been in the space that God ordained him to be, he would have recognized the signs. Month after month Rico and I spent more and more time (alone) together. We had lunch and sometimes dinner in each other's company. Our shops closed at the same time and on occasion, afterwards, we took walks together. Our relationship was more than sexual, we started to bond emotionally. We talked and laughed all the time. Rico would listen to what I had to say and he filled all the empty spaces in my heart.

About six months into the affair I realized that I was falling in love with him. I thought about Rico all the time. We started talking about leaving our spouses and moving in together. We spent as much time with each other as possible. When we were apart we talked secretly on the phone while in our homes. One and a half years flew by. Rico and I continued the affair. Oddly enough, of the many times that we had sex not only didn't we get caught (by our spouses) there weren't any close calls, either.

Then one night while Rico and I were at our homes talking on the phone to each other, his wife was listening in on our conversation. I do not know if she was growing suspicious or just by coincidence happened to pick up the other extension to dial out. After recognizing my voice, she yelled out, "Robin!" I immediately hung up the phone. Rico and his wife had a huge fight right then. She then drove over to my house. Thankfully

Lance was not home. She went off on me in front of my two young boys, "You're screwing my husband?" It was not a good scene. Rico arrived and after a few failed attempts he was able to get her away from my house. The first chance that she had she made sure that Lance knew firsthand what was going on.

Lance would have eventually found out for himself, but the inevitable finally happened. Lance confronted me about the affair. It was an ugly scene. I had never seen him so angry. He cursed up a storm. We argued back and forth.

I told Lance that I was in love with Rico. That angered him even more than he was. He hollered, "sleeping with another guy is bad enough, but you fell in love with this dude?" I felt terrible about what I had done. Lance was crushed. With a breaking heart he said, "How could you do this to me?" During Lance's outburst I became humbled and very apologetic. He then stormed out of the house!

Standing alone, sins exposed, I felt like a horrible person. The magnitude of my wrongdoing hit me square between the eyes. I thought, "Well, that's it, I finally ruined my marriage and family." I was an emotional mess, torn between wanting to keep my family together and yearning to be with Rico. Lance and I had been together for so many years, and there was a time that I considered him to be my best friend, but things had changed. A new man had captured my heart.

Chapter Eight

Divine Help

(Lance)

It was autumn 1986 when the crushing news of Robin's affair with Rico broke my heart. It did not surprise me that Rico wanted to have sex with my wife. She was young, beautiful and smart. I understood the mindset of a carnal man. I have to admit that even though I was angry and heartbroken, I had committed the same offense. Somehow I felt that me having sex with other women was different than Robin having sex with Rico. Sex was just sex, but she "fell in love" with Rico and that's what hurt the most.

Neither Robin nor I moved out of our house. We tried to live "life as normal" for our children's sake. That was difficult to do. Our home had always been peaceful. After hearing that she gave her heart to another man we argued every day. It was a very confusing time for the both of us. I wanted to keep our family intact but I wasn't so sure if Robin did because she continued to communicate with Rico. After the affair was out in the open she talked "freely" with him on our home phone while I was present. We continued a sexual relationship although I suspected that she remained intimate with Rico, too. To say that this was a confusing time in our marriage would be an understatement.

It would have been much easier if Robin and I had gone our separate ways. Dealing with her love for Rico was tough to handle. The pain tore me up inside. I felt as if my heart was being ripped out of my chest. The reason I didn't leave Robin was the fact that I couldn't abandon my family and I loved her.

Robin and I decided to let her parents know firsthand about the affair. They would have found out through the grapevine eventually. Being upfront with them was the right thing to do. I was very close to Mr. and Mrs. Mitchell. We had a great relationship. I had the best father and mother in-law that a man could have hoped for. The tremendous amount of respect that I had for Robin's parents weighed on me heavily because I did not want to lose their respect knowing that my marriage to their daughter was in jeopardy. After hearing about the affair they were very supportive and that was instrumental during our turbulent years.

I can vividly remember the disappointment Robin's mother expressed when we told them of Rico. She said with compassion, "Oh, Robin, Robin, Robin." I assured her parents, "We will work it out. I forgive her." Mr. Mitchell made a statement, "My parents were married for sixty-two years." He then looked at his wife, "We have been married thirty-four years. Divorce is not an option in our family and it is not part of our legacy. There is nothing that can't be worked out if you both want it, and with God all things are possible."

I remember when Robin and I had our first quarrel while (newly married) living in the Satinwood Street apartment. It was probably over something silly because I do not remember what we fought about. During the argument Robin stormed out of our home and said, "I'm going to my parents' house!" I gave her time before I headed over there, too. I wanted to get my wife back home where she belonged.

As I entered her parent's neighborhood surprisingly Robin was driving the opposite way. So I turned my car around and followed her. She pulled into a community park to talk with me.

I asked her, "I thought you were headed to your parents' house?"

She replied, "I did but once they heard why I was there they told me that my problem wasn't with them. They said my problem was at home and that is where I should be."

That is one of many great examples depicting the support that Mr. and Mrs. Mitchell gave towards my marriage and to their daughter.

The marital issues that Robin and I were having after the affair with Rico were seemingly insurmountable. I didn't know how to keep our marriage from ending in divorce, so I went to God and asked for help.

As a child, while living in Detroit, I attended summer bible school. At a young age I knew about God through children's biblical stories. As a teenager and into adulthood I didn't grow close to God. In fact, I did the complete opposite by living in sin.

Six months earlier when Robin came back from a women's church conference on fire for Jesus she asked if I wanted to start attending Loveland Church on a regular basis. At that time, I did not want to change my ways because I was having too much fun snorting cocaine, gambling in Las Vegas, and partying.

When my marriage was on the brink of divorce I came to God in desperation. I knew that my life had to change in order to keep Robin and my boys with me. Because of a failing marriage I was forced to turn away from my worldly ways and turn to God.

While on my knees, "Lord I need you. God, help me! I can't compete with Rico. She really loves him."

I heard God say in my spirit, "Yes you can. Just give me some time. I can fix your marriage if you trust me. Let Robin know how much you love her by regularly giving her flowers. Always give Robin something to look forward to like planning family trips." God provided me with a roadmap to heal my marriage, but He also let me know that it would be a difficult road for me to travel. He said if I didn't give up, He would perform a miracle in my life and my marriage! God was going to use our disobedience in marriage for His glory, but we didn't have a clue!

I continued in prayer for a long period of time seeking God for answers. It was then that I rededicated my life to Jesus. From that day forward I started a new and fresh relationship with God.

I became hungry to know everything that is written in the Bible. I approached a powerful man of God (Willie Hicks) from Loveland Church. He was an associate pastor. I asked him,

"What do I need to do to really understand the word of God?" His reply was very direct, "Here's what you do. Get yourself a Ryrie Bible, an exhaustive concordance, a bible dictionary and get to work."

In addition to doing all that Willie said I took it a step further. I converted one of the spare bedrooms in my house into a sanctuary with an altar. Every morning, sometimes as early as three o'clock, I got down on my knees in the sanctuary and prayed for long periods of time. During those precious times with God I also read the Bible. One of the first things that I prayed in my sanctuary, "God, if you fix my marriage I will serve you all the days of my life." When I make up my mind to do something I am "all in" and I was determined to do whatever was necessary to save my marriage. I had faith that Robin and I were going to make it!

It was then that I started to fall in love with Jesus. When I was in God's presence my marital issues seemed to go away. The sanctuary was an escape for me. My only focus was to stay in prayer and read the Bible. God was nurturing me by spoon-feeding me step-by-step and by giving me a road map back to Robin's heart.

At first she was indifferent when receiving flowers from me. Robin didn't believe that I was sincere in my motives but I did not let that stop me. I continued giving her flowers once a month and planned family outings, too. We took our boys on day trips to Disneyland, San Diego Zoo, to the ocean and camping at Silver Lake Park, as well as out of state vacations. It took a long period of time to win Robin's heart back. With

God's help we got through seven trying years before our marriage was back to normal again.

April of 1987 (six months after learning about the affair with Rico) my marriage wasn't getting better even though I was doing everything that God instructed me to do. During one of my early morning prayers that month I asked God, "What do I need to do to fix my marriage?" I heard in my spirit, "Take your family and leave the Rialto area." I did not want to uproot my family. Robin's parents lived only ten miles away. A few years back my mother and sister moved to Rialto, California from Detroit. They lived just two miles from my home.

A year and a half earlier I took an exam to become a sergeant with the Department of Corrections. I did not do as well as I thought I did on the test and because of that I was in the fifth rank. If I would have done better on the exam and been ranked first, second or even third then the California Rehabilitation Center (CRC) in Norco where I was working as a correctional officer would have hired me as a sergeant in a full-time position. They did offer me a temporary sergeant position but I wanted a long-term commitment.

I received many interview requests from various correctional departments within California but the locations were not in areas that I considered desirable. Most of the requests were from state prisons located in the California desert. I did not want to work that far away from Rialto and definitely not in a very hot climate.

In May 1987, shortly after hearing God say that I should move my family out of the Rialto area, I received a request for an interview in the mail. This time it was from the Richard J.

Donovan Correctional Facility (RJDCF) in San Diego County. It was a state prison that had just been built. I did not want to transfer my family that far away but I went just to see if I would get the position. My interview went very well. So much so, that by the time I got back home from San Diego I received a phone call from a lieutenant offering me a long-term sergeant position. I had to make a quick (on the spot) decision. With little time to think about uprooting my family I decided not to take this position and instead take a temporary sergeant position in Norco.

Immediately after hanging up the phone the Holy Spirit spoke to me again about moving my family out of Rialto and I knew that I had made the wrong decision by turning down the position in San Diego. My choice to stay in Rialto wrestled around in my spirit. I thought who wouldn't want to live in "beautiful" San Diego. Every correctional officer would love to work there. It is one of the most sought after areas. After the Holy Spirit convicted me for turning down that job, I thought, "It's too late they already gave the position to someone else." Once a position is turned down they quickly move to the next candidate on their list.

It was God's will for me to move my family to San Diego. It became crystal clear after an hour went by since hanging up the phone with the lieutenant from RJDCF. To my surprise I received another phone call from the same lieutenant.

He said, "You had a stellar interview and we want you as part of our team. Will you reconsider joining us?" No second-guessing this time around. I quickly replied, "When do you want me to report, sir?"

I only had thirty days before starting work at the Richard J. Donovan Correctional Facility. It is located just one and a half miles from the United States/Mexico border.

Fortunately, Robin's brother (Wayne), his wife Victoria (Tory), and infant son (Cameron), lived in San Diego County. I was able to stay with them in their two-bedroom apartment located in the City of Chula Vista. They lived twenty-minutes (north) from my new job. I drove back to Rialto on my days off. Robin and I put our house up for sale. She wanted to live in our home with the boys until it was sold.

Two weeks after moving to Chula Vista I received a phone call from Robin. She was very direct, "I'm not coming." I knew that her love for Rico had everything to do with the decision. I was furious, "What do you mean you're not coming?"

Robin, "I'm not coming!"

I quickly hung up the phone, dashed out of the house and drove to Rialto. During the long drive I dealt with gut wrenching pain and anger. What hurt the most was thinking that my family would not ever be together again. To my surprise Robin's tune had completely changed once I arrived home. She said, "I changed my mind." She then gave me a (loving) hug. I was not sure what had made her change her mind, but I was sure glad that she did.

Later in our marriage (during the healing and confessing stage) I learned that after Robin called me to say that she wasn't going to move she called Rico and asked him to come over. He did right away.

Robin said to him, "I made a decision I'm not leaving, so what are we going to do? The question took Rico off guard. Hesitantly he replied, "I need time to get things in order." Robin sensed that Rico had second thoughts. She got mad, "What are you talking about? You said that you wanted to be with me."

Rico looked at our family pictures on the fireplace mantle and remained silent. During a brief pause Robin filled with anger then hollered, "Get out! Get out of my house!" Rico left without another word spoken. I just so happened to arrive at the house a few minutes later. Of course I had no clue that Rico was just there. That's when Robin said to me that she changed her mind and decided to move to San Diego. During that period in our marriage things were crazy.

By September we had two offers on our house and it was time to pack up our Rialto home. Because I got a promotion to sergeant the State of California provided movers. We found a three-bedroom house to rent in the City of Santee (within San Diego County) located thirty-five minutes north/east of RJDCF. Robin closed her nail salon and as a family we moved together.

Robin did not look for work but instead she stayed home to raise and nurture our children. After Robin and I settled into our new home (far from Rico) I thought that her love for him ended but that was not so. Many nights she cried herself to sleep. On several occasions I held her in my arms to comfort her. My emotions were scrambled. I hurt knowing that Robin's heart was broken but it was over another man. The crazy times in our marriage just got crazier.

Robin's love for Rico was deeper than I imagined. I happened to look into her bedroom closet for something and came across a shoebox filled with photos of them, love letters and cassette tapes of songs that reminded her of him. I confronted Robin, "I can't believe you are still tripping over this dude. What, you got a shrine going on here? You still love this dude!" Robin was mad, "Why are you going through my stuff?" To make matters worse she kept the shrine despite the fact that I knew about it.

That occurrence took place about a year after Robin's affair was brought to my attention. After we moved to Santee I did not suspect that she was keeping in communication with Rico but I later found out that she was. Robin talked on the phone with him and on occasion they met in person.

Our marriage was still in turmoil. I kept reading the Holy Bible and prayed daily. One day at a time God brought me through that excruciating part of my life. During intimate times in prayer I found myself falling deeper in love with Jesus. He comforted my broken heart and gave me strength at the same time.

My (sergeant) position required working Sundays. That made it hard to attend church on a weekly basis. If I wanted a Sunday off I had to use a sick day or a vacation day. Although Loveland Church was in Riverside we continued to go there for several months until we found a church locally.

Our first church in San Diego County was Skyline Wesleyan Church. John Maxwell was the head pastor back then. We attended there for two years and became very involved with church activities.

The following year life continued on the same course. Our marriage did not improve. After our (Santee) lease ended, September 1988, my family and Wayne's family moved into a huge (six bedroom) house together in Bonita. Which is a lovely (fairly secluded) community within the city of San Diego. My drive to work was cut in half. A military couple owned the house and after the husband received orders to transfer out of California they rented the house to us.

It was a great situation for both families. We split the rent, utilities and household groceries fifty-fifty. Robin has always been close to Wayne and her sister in-law, Tory. I got along with them, too. The women did the grocery shopping. Wayne and I told them the money that they saved from each weekly grocery budget they could keep. That motivated Robin and Tory to became expert coupon clippers. The girls got so good at saving money that out of a three hundred dollar (weekly) grocery budget they would only spend half that amount. Wayne's family and mine spent a lot of time together. We did almost everything as joint-families, including going on vacations.

Spring of 1989 Robin and Wayne talked about participating on the "Family Feud" show. It was not long afterwards that the idea was put into action. Three members of the Mitchell family along with Robin and I drove to Hollywood for tryouts. Only five participants were allowed per family. We collectively agreed that Mr. Mitchell would be the head of the family. To his right stood Kenny, Wayne, me and last but not least, Robin. To our surprise, before the tryouts began, one of the show's producers informed us that families are chosen to do a "live show" based on how much excitement and fun that they had and not on wins and losses.

Just a few weeks afterwards we received a phone call informing us that our family was chosen to do a live "Family Feud" taping. We arrived on the specified day and time. The men wore suits and ties. Robin looked lovely, as usual. Shortly after arriving in the studio we were given some basic instructions then we played the game against the "Shine family." They won the previous game a day before. The first family that reached three hundred points wins the game and receives a monetary prize based on how many points that they earned. The family that wins goes on to play for "Fast Money" a chance for ten thousand dollars!

Richard Dawson (the original host of Family Feud) had retired four years earlier. Ray Combs was the host of the show then. We had a lot of fun during the live taping. It went by very fast.

After the first three rounds the Mitchell Family was up 115 - 89 points. The fourth round was my turn to stand at the front of the stage, where Ray stood, and go head-to-head against a member of the Shine family, Susan. Ray said, "The points are doubled. Top four answers are on the board. Name a female tennis player?" Susan hit her buzzer first and quickly answered, "Martina Navratilova." Which was the third answer on the board. I then answered, "Steffi Graf" she ranked fourth on the answer board.

The Shine family only had to guess the two remaining answers. If they got three strikes, then we had a chance to guess and hopefully steal the points. Their next answer (Chris Evert) was the top answer. After that the Shine family guessed three straight incorrectly. We had a chance for a steal. Ray started with Robin and went one-by-one up to Mr. Mitchell asking what answers we had. Robin was the only one that thought of someone, "Billie Jean King." Ray said to Mr. Mitchell, "You can choose an answer that your family gave or one of your own." He replied, "I am going to go with the beautiful girl on the end and say, Billie Jean King."

That was the last remaining answer. The Mitchell's led 265 – 89. Robin was next to go head-to-head with a member of the Shine family. Ray said, "Point values are tripled. Top three answers are on the board. Something someone hates to get into when it's cold?" Robin hit her buzzer first and answered, "Shower." That was the top answer on the board.

Only two remaining answers were left. Mr. Mitchell and Kenny did not answer correctly. Wayne did with "bed." It was then my turn. The pressure was all on me. If I guessed the last answer, then we would win the game. I said, "Handcuffs." Ray paused then repeated with a chuckle, "Handcuffs." The audience found my answer to be amusing, too because they had thought of handcuffs to be "kinky." When I realized that I explained, although I shouldn't have had to. Before the show started Ray met with each contestant and asked us something about ourselves. He asked me what line of work that I was in and I said, "Correctional Sergeant." With everyone continuing to laugh I said, "You know, when an inmate gets handcuffs put on it's cold?" There's nothing like getting embarrassed on national television. "Handcuffs" was not the last remaining answer.

That was our third strike. The Shine family had a chance to steal. Before their final answer was given Ray asked them to share all their answers. Three were given, "clothes," "car" and "outside air." The head of their family guessed "outside air" which was incorrect. The last remaining answer was "car." We won!

Our family decided that Robin and I would play for "Fast Money." Robin went off stage where she couldn't hear what Ray and I were saying. I stood up-front with my back to the answer board. The studio was extremely quiet. I gathered myself and focused on giving my best answer to five questions within fifteen seconds. Ray, "A letter of the alphabet that causes you trouble when playing scrabble? I quickly replied, "Z"

"A vegetable that you eat with your fingers?"

An immediate reply did not enter my mind. I briefly paused then said the first vegetable that came to my mind, "Broccoli."

"A food that comes on a stick?"

Without hesitation, "Popsicle."

"Name one of the Great Lakes?"

I am originally from Michigan so I better have had an answer to that question.

"Superior."

I answered all five questions with only a few seconds to spare. I turned around to see the results. If Robin and I (combined) reached two hundred points then we would win ten thousand dollars. My total score added up to one hundred forty-eight points. Wow! My answer "Z" scored thirty points and "Popsicle" (number one answer) forty-eight points. The audience, along with Ray and I, got a big laugh at my answer to vegetable (broccoli) that you eat with your fingers, which received zero points.

I walked over and stood next to the Mitchell family. Robin then walked into the studio. Ray informed her that she only needed to get fifty-two points. She had to answer the same five questions that I did. I knew Robin would accomplish that with ease. It took her just two answers to surpass two hundred points. Robin guessed (X) to the scrabble game question, which was the number one answer. She then said "Popsicle" as I did to the food on a stick question. Because of that Robin had to guess again and said, "Hotdog." Her first two answers totaled seventy-seven points. We were ten thousand dollars richer!

The Mitchell family divided up the total winnings, ten thousand five hundred and eight dollars, evenly. Because we won our family got another opportunity to play later that day. We lost the second game but celebrated all the way home for winning the first one.

After living in Bonita for fifteen months the owners of the house came back into town and my family, along with Wayne's family, had to move. We had a good thing going but such is life, things change. February of 1989 Robin and I bought a three-bedroom townhouse in Chula Vista. We enjoyed living there. Robin decorated our home beautifully.

When I became a sergeant, attending training programs was required. Some of the training took place out of town. In 1990 I participated in the Campaign Against Marijuana Planting (CAMP). The training spanned over a three-year period located in various parts of Northern California, sometimes for several weeks or months at a stretch.

During this time our marriage was still in survival mode. My time in prayer and reading the Bible was going strong but I was no saint. I still used cocaine and during two long training periods in Northern California I had causal sex with other women. I justified my sexual behavior as a mere "booty call." My thoughts at that time were self-centered, "Since there weren't any emotional attachments between me and the women that I had sex with, what was the harm? Unlike Robin with Rico."

I was growing as a Christian but I still had a lot to learn about living as a "Godly man." The more I relied on Jesus to help me in every area of my life the more "divine wisdom" I received and the more I matured.

Chapter Nine

Restoration

(Robin)

After Kashif was born Lance and I talked, several times, about having a third child. Both of us wanted a daughter. Adoption was the only way we could be certain that we wouldn't have another son. The winter of 1988 I said to Lance, "If we are going to adopt a girl let's do it now," he agreed.

We had to decide how old our daughter would be. Karama was just about to turn ten years old. He had plenty of friends. Being that Kashif was only four, Lance and I thought that it would be good for him to have a sister close in age to play with.

Adopting at this time in our marriage seemed like a good idea. Lance and I weren't arguing as much as we had been but our relationship was not flourishing either. Lance still liked to "party" which included a love affair with cocaine, and that bothered me a lot. God was working inside both of us and change was happening, but slowly.

After researching various adoption agencies in our area I contacted one that (primarily) cared for minority children, mostly African Americans. The same day that Lance and I submitted our application an agency worker let us look through binders full of children awaiting adoption. There were a lot more boys than girls to choose from. The daughter that I had in mind would resemble me, light skinned and with long hair. After viewing all the girls, I didn't see one that fit my description.

A few weeks later Lance and I were qualified by the adoption agency. I then called them and spoke with a woman. I ask her if any more girls had come in. She told me no. Her answer was a little disappointing, but I said okay. She then asked me if I had seen a little girl named Toneiquia. I thought I had. If Toneiquia was the girl that I was thinking of then she was four years old (same age as Kashif), tiny, cute, her hair was in pigtails, and she had on a pretty red and white dress. I did look at her picture, but she did not fill my requirements. The woman told me that they had a video of Toneiquia and asked if I would like to come down and take look at it. I knew in my heart that I should take a second look at her. I told the lady that I would come down to see the video.

When I arrived at the agency I looked through the binders one more time before watching Toneiquia's video. A girl that I did not remember seeing before caught my eye. She had a lot of my features and looked like she could have been my natural daughter. I excitingly said to an agency worker while pointing to the portfolio, "How about her? She's perfect!" The worker said that she was sorry, that the little girl had already been placed with another family. I was disappointed because I thought that I had just found my daughter.

I then viewed Toneiquia's video and learned that "TT" was her nickname. She was quiet, timid and very shy, which was the complete opposite of my personality. While listening to her talk on the video God spoke to my spirit, "You said you wanted a girl, this is your daughter." My heart softened and at that moment I knew that she was meant to be my daughter all along. On the drive home I thought about wanting a girl that resembled me and then I realized how superficial I had been. What I really wanted was a daughter to love and there she was, the daughter that God had for me. When Lance got home I gave him the good news.

The next step in the adoption process took place in early 1989. Lance and I went back to the agency and met with a social worker. She explained that first step was to meet TT in person to see if we wanted to adopt her. We decided that the local park would be a great neutral place to meet, however I let the social worker know that the meeting would not be the deciding factor. TT was already our daughter and the meeting was just a formality. Another family had recently rejected Toneiquia when she went to their home for a visit. The family was looking to add a little girl to their family that already consisted of a little boy. Toneiquia hit the little boy during the visit and they returned her to the agency stating that she would not be a good fit. How awful! Toneiquia already felt unwanted and then she was rejected too! I knew that we had enough love in our family to cover any hurts that she had experienced.

A few days later, Lance and I brought Karama and Kashif to meet Toneiquia. A social worker brought her to a park nearby our home. We spent about forty-five minutes together. Just like in her video she was very timid and shy. After introducing Toneiquia to her (soon-to-be) brothers and dad, she didn't want anything to do with them. She had no problem bonding with me. I greeted her with a hug, then pushed her on a swing. I tried to make her feel comfortable with light conversation. I asked Toneiquia what she liked and what she liked to do. She quietly spoke, "I don't know." I liked her nickname but I didn't want "TT" to stick with her when she got older. I thought Toni would be an appropriate nickname no matter what her age. I didn't want to take anything that was familiar to her from her without her consent, so I asked her if it was okay for me to call her Toni instead of TT? She said in her soft voice, "Yes." I knew that God brought her into our life for many reasons. Helping Toni get out of her shy shell was one of them.

The addition of Toni was a very exciting time in our family's life. Unfortunately, right after she met Lance for the first time, he was being sent to Northern California on special assignment for the C.A.M.P. (Campaign Against Marijuana Planting) program. It would require him to be gone for an extensive period of time. The adoption process was lengthy and before Toni was "officially" our daughter we had to share her with her foster parents.

Every morning I drove to Toni's foster parents house to pick her up so she could spend the day at our home, and at night I drove her back. I let her know that she was a part of the Croom family. I explained to Toni that she belonged to us just like Karama and Kashif. During our first drive back to the foster parents' house I let her know it was because "legally" I had to. I assured Toni that I was working on having her stay with us full-time.

Toni was very insecure from being bounced from one foster home to another. Because of that, I sensed she felt rejected and un-wanted, but not in our home. Toni became more and more comfortable after each visit. Karama and Kashif embraced her right away. The bond that Toni and I had from the beginning got stronger. Not just figuratively but physically, too, she clung to me wherever I went.

To my pleasant surprise, in less than a week of bringing Toni to our home, she did not want to leave. One evening when it was time for me to drive her back to the foster parents' house she got very upset. Toni cried out, "I don't want to go! I don't want to go!" I gave Toni a hug and assured her, "You are my daughter; it's just going to take a little longer that's all. You're a Croom, and we love you."

The next day I contacted the adoption agency and explained what Toni had said the day before. An agency worker explained the Foster Adoption Program to me and let me know we could keep Toni in our home full-time during the adoption process.

I was excited and Toni was too.

I was a little concerned about Toni not being able to bond with Lance since he was away on assignment during her (daily) visits. I decided to take all three children on a road trip to see him. After twelve long hours of driving with three children and all the (many) restroom stops we finally got there. The children and I stayed at a motel with an indoor swimming pool.

Toni had told me that she didn't know how to swim, so Lance and I kept a close eye on her and our two sons while they were splashing each other in the shallow end of the pool. Toni, holding fast to the sides of the pool was grabbed by her older brother and pulled away from the safety of the edge of the pool. She started to drift towards the deeper end, and when her feet could no longer touch the bottom of the pool she panicked. Lance immediately dove in and grabbed a hold of her. Toni wrapped her arms tightly around his neck and would not let go even when she was brought to safety. Lance became her hero and their bonding began from that moment.

Eight months later the adoption was finalized! At that time, I was not working. Being a stay-at-home mom helped me tend to Toni's needs. She developed low self-esteem while being in the foster care system. Maybe Toni lacked self-confidence because there was a lot of uncertainty in her future. Children need to feel secure, accepted and loved. She did not feel good about herself. Not only that but Toni was behind in school, too. Lance and I spent a lot of one-on-one time working on Toni's self-confidence and helping her catch up academically.

As a family we took Toni to places in Southern California that she had never been to before. San Diego has a long and beautiful coastline. Surprisingly, Toni said that she had never been to the beach. We sure changed that in a hurry! We took her to Belmont Amusement Park along Mission Beach. Other family outings included picnics at city parks where she met her extended family. She loved it! Especially when we took her to Sea World and Disneyland. Although slowly, those family adventures helped Toni come out of her shell.

Once Toni settled in and became fully acclimated to her new family, I decided to seek some adult interaction. The fall of 1989 and spring the following year I took (evening) classes, two nights per week, at Southwestern College. I took accounting, bookkeeping, and a math class. Although I loved being a stay at home mom, I needed some intellectual stimulation.

By 1990 our marriage wasn't thriving but Lance and I were surviving. Looking forward to special occasions helped us a lot. July 2, 1991 we celebrated our fourteenth wedding anniversary by spending two days at the historic (oceanfront) Hotel del Coronado. Before heading to Coronado, Lance stopped by the home of a friend of his to pick up some cocaine. His idea of celebrating our anniversary and my idea of celebrating was totally different. We arrived to our hotel room just in time to see a beautiful sunset. I thought maybe a romantic evening together would ignite a (much needed) spark in our relationship. That didn't happen. Once we settled in Lance displayed his stash of "coke" in perfect lines on the (glass) coffee table. I was angry and disappointed, too. I asked him, "Why do you need this?" He replied, "I don't, I like it." I put it bluntly, "You know, I'm losing all respect for you." Lance was stunned by my words. It took him a moment to reply, but when he did he humbly said, "Robin, I'm done with it." He then walked into the bathroom and flushed the cocaine down the toilet. I admired him for doing that but the atmosphere was adversely affected by his desire to get high. Very few words were spoken the rest of the night. While in bed Lance said, "Robin, you are more important to me than drugs." I then fell asleep in his arms feeling hopeful that God was making the necessary changes in both of our lives for a successful marriage.

The three-bedroom townhouse that we lived in was not big enough after Toni was added to our family. So, in September of 1991 we sold our home and bought an early 1950s ranch style four-bedroom house in Chula Vista. Lance and I still live there today. It is located in a family oriented neighborhood, which was perfect for raising our children. Having a backyard again has been nice. Karama, Kashif, and Toni made friends with other kids in the area right away. Toni and Kashif started attending Hilltop Elementary School located just down the street from our new home, and Karama attended Hilltop Junior High School right around the corner. Both schools were perfectly located to our new home.

After a few months of getting accustomed to our house, Lance and I decided that our children were responsible enough to have a puppy. They were thrilled! Lance took the children to a nearby residence where a litter of German Shepherds was being sold. Kashif, having a compassionate heart, wanted to pick the runt of the liter because the small male puppy looked scared and stayed in a corner by himself. The others were very hyper and aggressive. The runt looked so cute and sweet. After everyone came into agreement with Kashif, they brought the puppy home. Karama named our puppy "Suave" from a hit song at that time. I liked the name, too.

It didn't take the puppy long to become rambunctious and destructive. He chewed on everything, including our furniture, rugs, and he ruined our back yard irrigation system. I was furious! If he hadn't been so darn cute we would have put him on the next gravy train out of town. We loved Suave despite his puppy-destroyer tendencies and he became the furry addition to the Croom family. With a little training he calmed down but that didn't happen overnight.

By this time Toni was starting to come out of her shell. The first time that she spoke up for herself was when Suave urinated in her bedroom. I was annoyed because it was Kashif and Toni's responsibility to take Suave out to do his business.

I asked Toni why she didn't take Suave out and her reply was confidently stated. "It's not my fault. Kashif was supposed to let Suave out." My heart jumped for joy because our shy, timid child was standing up for herself. I grabbed her and hugged her. I couldn't stay mad at Toni after that. It was a milestone in her development and it made me so proud!

By early 1992 Lance was spending a lot of time reading the Bible and praying. He was up every morning, sometimes by three o'clock, spending time with Jesus in our den. I admired his devotion to God. Every day Lance told me stories from the Old Testament. He brought the characters to life by using animated expressions and voice tones.

Our marriage was showing some signs of improvement but not complete restoration. Lance and I were not talking to each other about our marital problems. In addition to that I still had feelings for Rico. We decided to see a marriage counselor.

I contacted a woman counselor near our home. Neither Lance nor I knew what to expect as we walked into our first session. To my surprise the counselor seemed to focus more on me than Lance. So much so that she scheduled a second session for just me, alone. She said that I acted cold and detached. I was quiet and aloof in our session, but that was because I was sizing her up just like she was sizing me up. I was offended by her assessment of me and had little confidence in her ability to help us.

On the drive home Lance and I got into an argument. As we were getting out of the car he said, "The more I hear you talk the more I know I can't please you." I sharply replied, "Then maybe you need to keep on trying! Or maybe we should just get a divorce?" Lance, being frustrated with me, agreed with the divorce part of my ultimatum. He said that he would transfer to a different institution because he could not live in the same city as me. He stated he would pay the house note and provide for the children. He then walked into the house without saying another word. I stayed outside to get some fresh air and to deal with fallout from the argument. How did we go from trying to get counseling to agreeing to divorce? The underlying issues kept raising their ugly head. As I tried to deal with the magnitude of the situation, I heard the voice of God speaking to my spirit. He said "I understand why you don't want your marriage the way it is, BUT if it could be how I designed it to be, would you want it then?" I had never thought about it that way before. Of course I wanted a marriage that honors God. I was losing hope that our marriage could be GOOD, but God gave me a new way of thinking. The light of hope flooded my heart and I became encouraged. God spoke to me again in his gentle, soft voice. "Give me your marriage and trust me. I will fix it!"

I went into the house and talked with Lance. I told him that I didn't want a divorce, he said he didn't either. We agreed that the only way our marriage would survive was for the both of us to surrender to God's will and make the necessary changes. We prayed, sought God for help, then put our "war strategy" into effect. We agreed our marriage was worth fighting for. Our fight was not with each other, we were fighting against forces that wanted to destroy not only our marriage, and our family but also our future influence to bless and minister to others. Lance and I first set up ground rules.

Rule #1 – Be honest with one another.

Rule #2 – Respect each other.

Rule #3 – Listen to each other.

Rule #4 – No excuses.

Rule #5 – Own your part.

Rule #6 – Pray.

Lance and I took daily (three to four mile) walks around the area that we lived in. We prayed together before, during and after each walk. Neither of us wanted to get a divorce. The Holy Spirit was with us every step of the way. Lance and I knew that our past couldn't hurt us unless we allowed it to. During those times together we talked about our marital problems, specifically the needs that weren't being met and how to resolve them. We discussed how we were going to make our marriage work. Lance and I needed to heal from the hurtful things that we did and said to each other throughout the (turbulent) years of our marriage. We confessed our sins and forgave one another.

God is amazing! It didn't take Lance and I very long to overcome our differences. Each walk was like steps of freedom. Every weight (frustration, expectation, guilt, shame, resentment, and anger) that held our marriage back lifted. Before Lance and I knew it we were practically skipping down the road, singing songs praising our Lord and Savior. After seven turbulent years, which tore our marriage apart, it only took two weeks for God to restore our relationship. We weren't perfect, but we were free! Some people find it hard to believe, but God's word is true. He is able, through his mighty power at work within us, to accomplish more than we can ask or think. What a mighty God we serve!

Chapter Ten

Ministry Leaders

(Robin)

God is faithful! He is Jehovah Jireh (the Lord who provides). God created a situation where Lance would surrender to His will. Lance wanted to give up his worldly ways, including gambling. In the fall of 1991 God led James, a friend of ours from Loveland Church to ask Lance if he would help with a church plant, by us being a part of the core group. The new church would be named New Dawn Christian Chapel, located towards the coast in Mission Valley. By accepting James' invitation, Lance and I would have to leave Skyline Wesleyan Church. At first when James asked Lance to come on board, his response was that he wasn't ready and he didn't think that God wanted him. Lance was changing but he still felt inadequate to be a part of leadership of any kind in any church. James was firm and stated that he had prayed about direction, and God had spoken his name along with fourteen others. After listening to James, Lance decided to accept the offer. The following year New Dawn Christian Chapel was open for worship.

God saw ahead of time the benefits that would come from Lance's commitment. God had a plan. Lance poured himself into his new responsibility. He was growing and he was growing fast, but there was one obstacle. Lance worked on Sundays. For a while he would take a personal day or vacation day to attend church on Sundays, but that became burdensome. Lance prayed that God would make a way for him to have Sundays off.

It wasn't long afterwards when the Department of Corrections offered Lance an Armory Sergeant position (teaching weapons training to correctional officers), which he accepted. His new job gave him weekends and holidays off! The blessing was two-fold. Besides being able to attend New Dawn Christian Chapel every Sunday, Lance had plenty of family time on the weekends and holidays, too.

Spring 1992 I went back to Southwestern College to take a Spanish and tennis class. Lance learned to play tennis when we lived in Rialto. He became an advanced player. Lance loved tennis! When we moved to Chula Vista he continued playing the game.

I believe that it is important for spouses to have some common interests. Friendship and camaraderie bring marriages closer. I wanted to spend more time with my husband, so I gave tennis a try. At first Lance didn't look forward to playing matches with me because I wasn't very good. But I was determined to get good enough so that Lance would want to play with me. That's when I decided to take a college tennis class. I caught on to the game very fast and earned a place on the college tennis team. More importantly, Lance started looking forward to playing with me.

Later that year I went with the tennis team to a tournament in Ojai, California, which is northwest of Los Angeles. The team stayed overnight in a motel. Because Lance had to work he couldn't watch me play. Although my marriage was restored I continued a friendship with Rico. We communicated from time-to-time over the phone. I did not want to sleep with him anymore. That part of our relationship had long been over.

Before going to Ojai I mentioned to Rico that I was excited to play in an upcoming tennis tournament. Rico said that he would come to watch me play. I knew that wasn't a good idea. Our bond was very strong. Every time we met in person the old feelings that I had for him resurfaced. I just knew he would try to persuade me into having sex, but I felt strong enough to resist. Rico drove to Ojai and just as I thought, we wound up being intimate.

Afterwards I was so disappointed with myself for not being strong enough to withstand his advances. I didn't let Lance know about the one-night-stand with Rico. I felt guilty for my actions and felt that I had let God down. I had so much self-condemnation. How could I have sinned against God again after all that he had done for us? My heart was broken because I broke God's heart! Why would I risk the same consequences as before? How could I have let that happen? Why did it happen? So many questions reverberated in my mind. As I worked through all my emotions, God reassured me that I was still His. He told me to get up and not do that again. He let me know that I had made the decision to do wrong, and I put myself in a position that led to my wrong choice. When God delivers you from anything, you cannot look back, you cannot dabble in it thinking you are strong enough to resist. The devil knows your weakness and he is more than happy to use it against you. My advice is to resist the devil and he will flee. Don't give the devil a foothold. I learned many lessons from that experience, but the most important one was that God had not given up on me and he was giving me another chance! I knew that I had to pour myself into Him, the One that loved me like no other. There was still work that needed to be done!

I worked alongside Lance at New Dawn Christian Chapel. It was exciting to be involved in starting a church. In addition to that, I attended a weekly (woman's) International Bible Study Fellowship (BSF) group in Chula Vista. I received a lot of revelation from the Holy Spirit during those meetings. While attending a BSF meeting the Holy Spirit convicted me of my platonic relationship with Rico. I knew then that I had to break off all ties with him.

Confusing feelings for Rico wrestled around inside of me for hours that day. My thought process was wrong and I needed to change my mind if I wanted to change my actions. I wanted God to allow me to have a friendship with Rico knowing that even that was a crazy thought. My heart broke thinking that Rico and I would never talk to each other again. The Holy Spirit told me that even the smallest amount of communication between Rico and me would be too much.

Later that day, while at home, I painfully prayed to God, "Take away the feelings that I have for Rico. I do not want them anymore." I then called him to end our relationship (for good). I said sadly, "It is very hard for me to say this but please do not call me anymore." It was difficult for Rico to release me all together, so he tried to hang a guilt trip on me in an effort to persuade me into changing my mind. Rico's reply was smooth, "You said that we would always be friends – right?" His sly tactics worked on me before but not this time. I had to obey God! After hearing Rico's futile attempt, I knew I could end all communication with him. With a lump in my throat I said, "If you love me, like you say you do, then you will let me go." Rico softly spoke, "Okay."

With relief I said, "Thank you."

That was it! God gave me the strength to end my seven-year relationship with Rico, physically and emotionally. As I look back, I was deceived to give another man the loyalty that belonged only to my husband. My mind was really messed up. The more I focused on God's word and His truth, the more my mind cleared and my thinking began to be more focused.

My marriage continued getting stronger. Lance and I enjoyed going on family vacations, having backyard barbeques, taking our children to the beach and city parks. Often we would drive to Rialto to visit family.

I didn't have to work, because Lance was making good money, but I wanted to. Any extra income would come in handy. I thought about what my next business adventure could be. Our housewarming party on King Street came to mind. I did the cooking and my sister-in-law, Tory, decorated. All of our guests had a great time! Some asked, "What caterer did you hire?" They were pleasantly surprised when I said that I did the cooking. After hearing a lot of positive feedback on how well the party went it dawned on me then that I could do this for a living.

Late 1992 Tory and I started discussing going into a catering business together. We agreed that there was a market for it. After putting our heads together, we started C & M Custom Party Planners by February of the following year. C & M came from the first letter in each of our last names. I did the food preparation (cooking and baking) and Tory made everything look good. We took all the necessary steps in applying for a business license. We had business cards printed, which helped promote work by word of mouth. It was very exciting!

Early on most of our customers just ordered birthday and wedding cakes. On a hunch one day, I decided to stop into Roller Skateland. I knew that they held birthday parties there. I thought, "Someone had to be making the cakes." I approached the manager and asked, "Who makes your birthday cakes?" The manager mentioned a bakery nearby.

I continued, "I have a party planner business and I would like to bring you some samples." The manager accepted my offer as he told me he was becoming dissatisfied with his present bakery. On that note I hustled home and whipped up two cakes (white and chocolate) and brought them down to the rink. The manager liked the cakes and I got our first contract. Roller Skateland was loyal to my business for many years until they retired their business.

By early 1994 Lance and I were looking for another church. New Dawn Christian Chapel dissolved within two years. The church did not live up to its full potential, and we were led to another church that too would not be our final destination. We attended Skyline Wesleyan church for two years, gaining a firmer spiritual foundation, but soon we were looking for another church that would serve the needs of our entire family.

After visiting many churches in our area none of them seemed right for us. During our search Lance remembered, not too far back, that I had catered a small event for New Creation Church. He reminded me of how impressed I was with the people of that church. After arriving home from delivering the food I said to Lance, "I like the people there. One day I would like to visit."

So, we visited New Creation Church the following Sunday. We were used to serving at our other churches in one capacity or another and we both were looking forward to finding our niche at New Creation. Lance and I enjoyed getting involved with church functions. Not long after attending our new church Lance joined the choir and I got involved with special events. My first project was a fashion show fundraiser.

God opened up more opportunities for Lance and I to serve. As a way to befriend other married couples and to strengthen our marriage we attended "Honeys N Harmony" a marriage ministry at church. We quickly made many wonderful friendships. After attending Honeys N Harmony for the first time Lance and I felt like this was a ministry that God wanted us to serve. Well, it didn't take long for that to happen. Six months later the married couple that led the marriage ministry had to step down. They were re-locating out of town and would no longer be attending New Creation Church. During our participation in the group, Lance and I had the opportunity to share our testimony of restoration with them. When they knew they were leaving they excitedly shared with the others in the group, "We found someone to take over the ministry!" While God was fixing our marriage, He was preparing us for ministry to help other marriages. God's plans are perfect!

Something fun happened to me in the spring of 1994. My brother Wayne informed me that he wanted to try out to be a contestant on the "American Gladiators" (TV) show. He was a six-foot one-inch bodybuilder with bulging muscles. The contestants were amateur athletes in excellent physical condition. Wayne resembled the muscular physique of the "Gladiators" more than a contestant.

Two contestants competed against one another. The winner received two thousand five hundred dollars and a spot in the Champion Tournament. Points were earned by competing in contests challenging their strength and agility. During the first six competitions contestants were challenged by highly skilled and extremely strong "Gladiators," then they faced-off against each other in the last challenge. An audience circled the "Gladiator Arena" during the live taping.

My parents, Tory, and I, along with our children, wanted to watch Wayne during the tryouts. We gathered at my parents' house early in the morning before heading to Hollywood. Wayne asked me several times if I wanted to tryout too. Female contestants competed against each other and woman Gladiators. I wasn't sure if that was a good idea. I kept myself fit but I wasn't in prime (athletic) condition now at thirty-seven years of age. Most of the contestants were in their twenties and early thirties.

I asked Wayne what were some of the requirements to qualify. One of the challenges mentioned was to complete ten pull-ups by locking out the elbows before each one. I thought that I could but I wasn't sure. My parents had one of those old clotheslines in the backyard, so I went out back and used the side post to testy my strength. I was able to do ten! Even though I wasn't completely convinced I was in good enough shape to pass all the tests, I told my brother I would try out too! Wayne and I had to wait in a very long line before getting a chance to try out. There were over two thousand (hopeful) contestants ahead of us and because of that it took three hours before we got in. It was hard staying loose after standing on my feet for such a long period of time, but the line did move quickly.

The first challenge of the tryouts was pull-ups. I struggled locking out my arms before each pull-up, so did Wayne. I do not know why, I did them correctly at my parents' house. Neither of us was allowed to move on to the next challenge. Wayne went back in line to try out one more time. I wasn't so enthusiastic about doing that again. I waited with my family for Wayne to go through the line a second time. There were a lot less people waiting this time around. Within a half an hour Wayne was close to getting in again. He then said to me, "Come on, try it one more time." I replied, "Okay, okay, I'll do it again." I walked in with him.

This time Wayne and I made it through the pull-ups. Every test after that consisted of running, jumping, or climbing. We became more and more determined to complete the tryout after passing each physical challenge. By the time it was over every muscle in my body ached and my legs felt like rubber, but I was thrilled to have finished!

The next phase was an interview. One of the questions asked: "Why do you want to be on American Gladiators?" That was an easy question. My reply, "I want to show women, that no matter how old they are, they too can be a contestant on The American Gladiators. They can do anything that they put their mind to." The interviewer said, "Towards the end of tryouts we could tell that you ran out of a gas." While laughing at what was just said I replied, "Yes, I did run out of gas, I was exhausted."

Interviewer, "Well you know, if we pick you to be on the show you would have to do some training." I replied, "That wouldn't be a problem. My brother is here and he will train me. I didn't even come up here to be on the show. It was just on a whim. I didn't do any training ahead of time. I just came up because my brother was coming to try out." The Interviewer wrapped it up with, "Okay, we'll call you if you are selected to be on the show."

About a week later I received a phone call from a producer, "You have been chosen to be on the show. You will be the oldest female contestant to ever be on American Gladiators." I got very excited! Wayne did not get selected. Since he was a trained bodybuilder and just as big and strong as the Gladiators the producers suggested that Wayne try-out to be one of the gladiators, but he wasn't interested.

Wayne said to me, "I'm going to train you sis." I intensively trained for three months during the summer before going on the show. A lot of the training took place at Southwestern College where Wayne had me run up and down the football stadium stairs. The first time I gasped for air over and over again, and felt like I was going to die. I was determined to get into shape to compete on the show. I didn't give up not even once. Even if I wanted to, Wayne would not let me. After running the stadium stairs Wayne had me do fifty-yard sprints on the football field then go immediately into push-ups. In addition, Wayne trained me in a gym, too. I had to run a lap around the track, then workout on cardio machines and lift weights, as well as abdominal exercises (sit-ups and crunches). Oh, man, he worked me out! I was pushing forty years old and I got into the best shape of my life.

During the training I continued to work with Tory at our catering business and be at home for my children and husband. That was a very busy time in my life!

Before the scheduled show I had to go to Hollywood to train for a week on the show's apparatuses. They paid for my hotel and food. Tory called me while I was away and said that she didn't want to work in the business any longer. I understood why. Business wasn't steady and most of our customers just wanted party platters and cakes delivered, which I made. There weren't that many opportunities for Tory to use her designer/decorator talents.

My entire family came to watch me compete on "American Gladiators" live taping. I was so nervous that day. Because my stomach was in knots I couldn't eat a meal. I was only able to drink water and energy drinks, as well as snack on power bars. The producers provided a color coordinated tank top and shorts to wear. They also gave me a helmet, knee and elbow pads, I was ready for battle! Two shows were taped in one day, which turned out to be a good thing. The downtime provided moments of rest in-between challenges. That was needed because the Gladiators beat up on me pretty good. It also gave my fellow contestant (Lorraine) and I time to talk. I learned that she lived in California, was only two years younger than me, and a mother of five young children.

The first competition (Powerball) Lorraine and I competed against the Gladiators at the same time. We had forty-five seconds to pick up as many small red balls (one-at-a-time) as we could and drop them into one of five larger bins that were evenly spread out. Each ball that was dropped into a bin equaled a point. Lorraine and I ran as fast as we could (zigzagging) around the Gladiators. They knocked us around and sometimes dragged us down to the ground. I was able to score two points. Lorraine wasn't able to score. Man, was I tired and bruised after that!

The next two contests I didn't score any points and Lorraine built a sizable fifteen to two lead. During the second challenge (Whiplash), a form of tug of war against a Gladiator within a large (padded) ring, my hand slipped off the device that we held together, with only one hand. I was upset with myself for that. Lorraine was able to pull the Gladiator out of the ring and received ten points.

Next up was a race called Sky Track, which took place (upside down) on the ceiling. There were three tracks, Lorraine and I on the outside and a Gladiator was in the middle. Harnessed in, we raced side-by-side using our hands and feet to go down a (multiple s-turn) track and back. Wow did I get dizzy! The (more experienced) Gladiator got to the end of the track first and quickly made her way towards us after turning around to race back. As I was going by her she reached out and made a grab for my foot, which slowed me down. If it weren't for that I might have come in second place but Lorraine did by inches and earned five points.

The fourth competition (Slingshot), long bungee cords were attached to our waists. Lorraine and I had sixty seconds to score as many points as we could by placing balls into bins. The bins were located on platforms attached to tall poles. We continuously leaped off the platforms grabbed balls (in one motion) from the pole and with the help of our bungee cords jump back up to the platform for a score. Of course the Gladiators wore bungee cords, too. Three of them tried to prevent us from scoring. I came away with four points. Lorraine wasn't able to score. My legs hurt so much after that!

Our fifth contest (Assault) consisted of hitting a far-away target using a crossbow with plastic arrows and three (futuristic looking) guns with rubber bullets within one minute, while a Gladiator shot at us with a similar style gun. Lorraine and I took separate turns. It was tricky because we had to duck behind objects so not to get hit but also find time to shoot at the target. I scored six points to Lorraine's five. She had a twenty to twelve lead.

Our sixth challenge (Joust) required the two of us to compete against a Gladiator at different times. We stood on a small (round) platform high off the ground supported by a narrow base and held a lance (pole) with cushioned ends, like a huge Q-tip swab. A Gladiator faced-off against us standing on an equally high and rounded platform, also holding a lance. Ten points were given by knocking the (very experienced and strong) Gladiator off her platform or five points by holding our ground resulting in a draw within the thirty-second period of time.

Lorraine went first, not only was she able to withstand an onslaught of hits but she knocked the Gladiator off balance just enough to score ten points. Gladiators do not like to lose and they get pretty mad the (few) times that they do. Well, that didn't bode well for me because the same (ticked-off) Gladiator that just lost to Lorraine faced-off against me. She came at me with a vengeance. I wasn't able to land many hits on the Gladiator but I did stand my ground for (almost) the entire time. Oh it was so close! The Gladiator knocked me off balance with two seconds left on the clock. I tried to keep from falling off but to no avail, my feet went airborne with only one second remaining. Darn! Lorraine had a thirty to twelve lead.

The final competition (Eliminator) did not involve the Gladiators. Lorraine and I ran side-by-side along an obstacle course. The winner won the prize money. Because Loraine had an eighteen-point lead she got a nine second head start. This (final) leg of the contest was referred to as "The Great Equalizer" because (as in my case), although Lorraine had a sizable lead I had a chance to not only catch up with her but also win the contest.

At the sound of a whistle Loraine was off, she climbed two stories using an Armitron (looked like an extremely large

Stairmaster). I didn't know nine seconds could seem like ninety minutes. By the time I started up the Armitron Lorraine was already onto the second segment, going down a huge slide. Before I could get to the slide she started the hand-bike challenge. Halfway across Lorraine fell off and incurred a penalty. She had to wait ten seconds before moving onto the next obstacle. Her mishap gave me a chance to catch up. That I did! Because I had no problem on the hand-bike Lorraine and I were neck and neck on the fourth challenge. We had to make our way across a long (spinning) cylinder. Lorraine fell off that, too, but no penalty was given. Her second mistake gave me the lead right before I climbed a very tall cargo net. By the time I reached the top Lorraine had just begun to climb.

From high above the obstacle course I could hear my family cheering me on through the (loud) audience. That gave me strength! I grabbed onto a bar with two hands and quickly zip-lined down to the ground. I was on a roll! Momentum was building. The next challenge required a climb up a Plexiglas wall using a rope. My legs and arms started to give out on me right then. I knew that I had a lead, so I took a little time before making a running start. After a deep breath I ran and leaped onto the wall while grabbing a hold of the rope but I couldn't get enough leg and arm strength to hoist myself over the top.

Lorraine had just finished the zip-line and was making her way over. I was in worse pain after that last attempt but I had to try again (right away) because Lorraine was fast approaching. My second attempt wasn't good enough either. I stood bent over in pain. The wall blocked out my family's voices because they were seated behind it. I couldn't hear them cheering me on anymore. If I would have heard Wayne yell out, "Get over that wall Robin! Get over that wall!" that would have strengthened me to conquer the challenge.

Before my third attempt Lorraine passed me by getting over the wall on her first try. That motivated me to leap onto the wall one-more-time and with every bit of energy left in me I made it over the top, barely. By this time Lorraine was making her way up a very steep treadmill. I was determined to make up lost ground. So I put all thoughts of pain and fatigue aside and charged up the treadmill. It didn't take me long to get within a few steps of her. Lorraine got to the top first and then after grabbing a long rope swung herself over the finish line dropping onto a blue mat below. A mere two seconds was all that separated us by the time I landed on the mat, too. Lorraine and I lay on the mat in exhaustion not moving a muscle.

A woman from the show came over to congratulate Lorraine and to do a quick interview with her. We got up from the mat then stood side-by-side holding hands. The woman asked Lorraine, "What do you have to say?" While still catching her breath Lorraine looked into the camera and said, "This is for all the older woman out there. You can do it! You can do it!" My sentiments exactly...

After that amazing experience my life (quickly) went back to normal. Things were going along smoothly. My marriage was good and our children were happy. C&M Custom Party Planners was growing, but slowly. I wanted to keep busy all the time. In addition to catering I started work at the Richard J. Donovan

Correctional Facility as an office assistant. I enjoyed working with the personnel. For all the office parties I baked cakes and other treats, which in turn increased my catering business. My coworkers enjoyed the food so much that they started ordering from me for their (home) parties.

In 1996, for some strange reason, I got Bell's Palsy. It caused muscles on the left side of my face to weaken to the point of paralysis. On my way to a church ministry meeting I suddenly got very tired. My eyelids felt heavy. I dismissed it as being overly busy. The meeting took place around a large table. Not long after sitting down I became very sleepy and rested my head on the table. I heard someone say, "Are you okay?" I knew something was very wrong. I asked them to get Lance who was also at the church, for choir rehearsal. As soon as Lance saw me he too knew something was wrong. We rushed to the emergency room. After seeing a doctor, I was told it could have come from a cold virus. Bell's Palsy usually goes away within six weeks but if it doesn't go away by then there could be some residual facial weakness. I didn't let fear get to me. God is Jehovah Rapha (my healer) and in Him I trust. Lance and I prayed together for healing.

My (partial) paralyzed face didn't keep me from attending church. The following Sunday I thought about not going. I said to Lance, "Go without me but save a seat in case I decide to show up." I didn't want people to see me in that condition. I had no facial expressions on the left side of my face. To make matters worse the doctor gave me an eye patch because my left eye would not close on its own. What a pretty sight I was. While in bed that morning I heard the Holy Spirit say to me, "Get up and go." Although I didn't want to, I got up anyway. Dressed in all black (reflecting my mood) I headed to church.

Once there I spotted Lance right away. He sat up front where we usually did. That was the longest walk of my life. I tried to show no emotions whatsoever so the distortion of my face wouldn't show. I knew that the left side of my face wouldn't smile when the right did. Holding back emotions was all but impossible to do. The right side of my face started to move; then tears rolled down my face. I felt as if everyone's eyes were on me. At that moment I felt compassion for anyone that had a physical deformity. One reason Lance and I joined New Creation Church was because the people there were so loving. I was blessed by their outpouring of love that day. As an Altar Worker I stood my post and prayed for those who came to the altar for prayer, despite the fact that I had to wipe the drool from my chin frequently. The hearts of many were touched by my courage to face life during this time of adversity.

God did heal me and my life was back on track. Praise the Lord! God taught me many life lessons through the process. About seven weeks after getting Bell's Palsy I started experiencing excruciating headaches that were worse than migraines. I thought, "On top of everything else I have to get headaches, too?" Through the difficult ordeal God said to me, "Pain is part of the healing process." I believe the pain was telling me that healing was on the horizon. Soon afterwards I felt a twitch on the left side of my face. I quickly ran to a mirror to look at my face to see if there was any sign of improvement. There was! Ever so slightly I could see the (once paralyzed) part of my face move. Talk about encouraging! My heart soared as tears rolled down my cheeks. This time the tears were in gratitude and of hope. I was able to minister to many couples who were experiencing the pain of betrayal in their marriage! I encouraged them not to give up when it got hard. They would experience pain, yes, but healing would be on the horizon! It's always the darkest before the dawn, and the bright morning star (Jesus) shines the brightest right before the dawn. Don't give up!

Chapter Eleven

Only God

(Lance)

God had done a great work in my marriage. I give Jesus the praise, honor and glory for healing and strengthening my relationship with Robin. Twelve years after learning of Robin's love affair with Rico, I welcomed him and his wife, Terri, into our home. The summer of 1998 Rico called my house (mid-day) out of the blue to say that he and his wife had something they wanted to give Robin and me. Rico mentioned that he and Terri were driving back to Rialto after spending the day in Tijuana (Mexico) and since they were going to drive through Chula Vista he asked if it was okay if they stopped by. I was cool with that, "All right. Come over." After hanging up the phone I let Robin know. She seemed a little apprehensive, but I wasn't.

Upon entering our home Rico and Terri gave us a very nice gift. It was a large black version painting of "The Last Supper." Robin and I thanked them for their generosity. We asked Rico and Terri to make themselves comfortable in our living room. Robin brought out refreshments. After a short period of small talk we moved on to talking about our past and how incredible it was that we were all together in our living room after everything that had transpired.

Terri spoke and said, "I know that Rico really loved Robin, and he is a better man for knowing her."

I could sense Robin was a bit uncomfortable and Terri's statement caught her off guard.

Robin, sympathetic, said, "I'm sorry for hurting you. I wish I could go back and change things."

Terri replied graciously, "I have forgiven you and Rico too."

Rico then looked at me and apologized too.

"You know man, I'm really sorry."

My reply was truthful; "I never held it against you."

The four of us spent a couple of hours together and during that time our conversation flowed smoothly. We talked like we were old friends. I was glad that Rico and his wife stopped by. I will never underestimate the power of forgiveness. God can and will restore all the years we allow the devil to consume. What was once broken seemingly beyond repair, God fixed. God gave final closure to a time in our life that was filled with heartache and pain. We were free to move forward to the next chapter on our journey of life.

Chapter 12

The Business

(Lance)

Life was good. Robin kept busy with C&M Custom Party Planners while working at RJD. I wasn't too involved in her catering business, although she wanted me to be. I helped her from time-to-time but I found out later that Robin had regularly prayed for me to get on-board. April of 1999 Robin thought about opening a bakery because most of her business came from her baked goods. Our kitchen was too small for the amount of orders that she was getting. I helped by spending a couple of Saturdays driving Robin around to vacant storefronts in Chula Vista.

Little by little God was removing those things in my life that didn't honor Him. Another removal was about to take place. At that time in my life I still smoked cigarettes, which bothered Robin a lot. A few years before, I made a New Year's resolution to quit, but didn't. On one Saturday as we were looking for a store for lease, I pulled out a cigarette. Robin gave me an annoyed look and said, "I thought you were going to quit?" I got angry and snapped at her, "Look, don't sweat me! I'll quit when I am ready to quit!"

By the disappointed look on Robin's face I knew her feelings were hurt. The Holy Spirit immediately convicted me for speaking to her in that manner. I heard God say in my spirit,

"Look you were the one who told her you were going to quit smoking and now you have the audacity to get mad at her because she is trying to hold you accountable to your word. Why would you get mad at her?" I knew I was wrong. Tears welled up in my eyes as I apologized. "You know what baby? I'm sorry for the way that I spoke to you. I was totally out of line, and I am going to quit smoking!" I then reached into my jacket pocket, pulled out the pack of cigarettes, crumbled it in my hand and threw it away. That night I prayed, "Lord Jesus, I smoke because I enjoy smoking. It relaxes me. It gives me a sense of well-being. It's something that I feel the need to do, but it is something that doesn't bring you honor. I don't smoke around church members or around my kids, so you know that I am ashamed of it. It's bigger than me. I need you to take the desire away from me." Later that night while in bed, I shared my prayer with Robin. Ever since that prayer I never had the urge to light a cigarette again. One more thing that God took out of my life. Moving forward!

The cost to lease a store was more than we could afford at the time so we didn't open a bakery. May of 2000, C&M Custom Party Planners got a major break. Robin was offered an opportunity to be the sole food vender at the Pacific Coast Open Tennis Championship (USTA). San Diego hosted the tournament that year. Robin and I were members of the Mountain View Tennis Club at that time. We made a lot of friends there. Some of the members from the club were responsible to find food vendors. They knew of Robin's catering business and asked her if she would like to sell food from the concession stand. Robin said, "Yes!" We quickly learned that we would need a million-dollar liability insurance policy in order to sell food at the venue. We weren't sure if that was affordable. Robin started calling around for quotes. One of the insurance agents that she contacted was Jerome. As it turned out he was a member of our church but we didn't know it at the time. Jerome said it would cost us approximately six hundred dollars for the policy we needed. Robin did her homework and got other quotes, several lower in cost, but she chose Jerome's company because he was a member of our church. Six hundred dollars was a lot of money for us at the time, but Robin and I agreed to step out in faith and pay it. After Jerome calculated all the numbers the premium turned out to be less than his initial quote, and all the other quotes she received as well. God blessed us for stepping out in faith. After Robin signed the insurance forms Jerome mentioned to her that once a week he provided lunch to the employees at several Ford Dealerships in the area. The dealerships were insurance clients of his. He then said to Robin, "Let's talk business. I'm going to need a quote for some catering." Robin asked him what he had in mind and how many people he needed served. After receiving the information, she quoted him almost the exact amount that the insurance premium cost us. God was really blessing us and opening huge doors of opportunity! Jerome continued ordering lunches for the dealerships (through Robin) for many years after that.

C&M Custom Party Planners got a lot of exposure during the tennis tournament. Throughout the three-day event the concession stand kept very busy. With my help, as well as our children (Karama was 21 years old, Kashif and Toni both 16 at the time) we managed to make a good profit. That weekend wasn't all work because Robin and I had fun competing in the tournament too. We played a doubles match but weren't able to advance to the next round. I then played a singles match and won but lost to the next opponent. All in all, the weekend was a great experience and a great success!

Later that same year my Aunt Sonia mailed me a cassette tape of a sermon from Pastor Chuck Singleton of Loveland Church. The message was titled "Millionaires." I listened to it. Pastor Chuck read many scripture pertaining to "hearing the calling of God for your life and then doing it." Two of the Bible verses that he used came from Romans 12: 4 and 5:

"For as we have many members in one body, but all the members do not have the same function.

So we, being many, are one body in Christ, and individually members of one another."

Pastor Chuck went on to say, "God has a plan for each man and some are called to be millionaires for the purpose of furthering God's Kingdom. Don't miss out on what God has for you." He also mentioned, "Henry Ford and Alexander Graham Bell followed through with what God called them to do and you know what they accomplished." Pastor Chuck further explained, "The richest place on earth is the graveyard because many were buried with God's plan in their mind but they never followed through to complete it." He said, "Some people became complacent with where they were in life and they were too afraid to leave their job to pursue what God had placed in their hearts to do. So instead of being abundantly blessed and blessing others, they died without fulfilling the purpose that God had for their life."

At that time in my life I believed God had been telling me to be prepared to leave the Department of Corrections, but I didn't share that with Robin. In September 2000, not long after listening to Pastor Singleton's sermon, God gave me a vision for Robin's catering business. To my surprise it included me. The vision came on a Sunday (early morning) as I was sitting in my living room studying the word of God. I envisioned a legacy and wealth that Robin and I could leave for our children. In my mind I saw many trucks with our last name written on the side. God also gave me the motto for the business "Quality, Care, Integrity and Love of Service." A couple of hours later, after giving it some thought, I awoke Robin from her sleep to share the vision with her. She became very excited! That's when Robin told me that she had been praying for me to get involved with the catering business. Her prayers were answered.

I continued working at RJD and helped Robin with catering orders on the weekends. My approach to work and Robin's were very different. We had some adjusting to do – to say the least. Because Robin had been running the business for seven years by herself she had many systems already in place. Robin meticulously planned out every catering order ahead of time. I didn't work that way. My style was the opposite of hers. I thought, "What difference does it make how it gets done as long as it gets done on time." Robin took the time to show me how she did things. Because I had no say (I didn't know anything about what she did), I reluctantly and grudgingly went along with it. My style, which sometimes got things done at the last minute, clashed with her perfectly "preplanned" scheduling. Since both of us are strong willed and leaders, a lot of friction formed between us. Early on it was like oil and water. Over time and after many arguments we worked out a system that benefitted the both of us. We allowed God to be CEO and we operated in our strengths. We respected the gifts and talents that each of us brought to the table, and learned to appreciate the intricate balance it takes to work together in unison. Keeping it real, it's not easy to work with your spouse, but it is POSSIBLE!

I liked to jog around my neighborhood. It gave me alone time with God. He usually spoke to my spirit during those times. While on a jog in early December of 2000 I heard in my spirit that I should quit my job as a lieutenant at RJD and work full-time with my wife. When I hear from God I do not waste time. Once arriving home I looked Robin eye-to-eye with all seriousness and said, "I'm going to quit my job and work with you." It must have taken her by surprise because her response was "WHAT?"

Robin said that she prayed that I would get more involved in the catering business, but she didn't expect me to quit my job. Robin asked me if I prayed about my decision. I told her that God spoke to me during the jog and placed this on my heart to do. As the primary financial supporter for my family I knew that giving up my lieutenant's salary would be a huge leap of faith. On top of that I wasn't fifty years old yet so I couldn't receive a pension. God spoke something else to my spirit during that jog, "It will be one of the hardest things that you will ever do, but with faith and hard work you can accomplish anything." I didn't understand at the time what I would have to go through.

It didn't take Robin long to trust my decision because she said God gave her a peace and confirmation. She was on board. Some of our family members thought I was crazy to leave RJD with only eight years left before being eligible for retirement. I didn't let their doubts bother me. Sometimes God will have you do things that don't make any sense to anyone else. Robin became very excited about the possibilities that awaited us and so was I! That's all that mattered to me.

Things moved quickly from that moment on. I communicated to Robin that when we got a location for the catering, we might as well open a restaurant too. At first she wasn't on board with that idea because she knew how many hours her parents spent running their restaurant and that didn't appeal to her. After some convincing Robin agreed.

We decided to specialize in barbeque and home-style cooking. Chula Vista didn't have many restaurants like that. Robin and I started looking at storefronts again. This time the commercial space would be for a restaurant, which would include catering and a bakery. I figured we could afford to lease space this time because the restaurant by itself would generate a lot of money; the catering and bakery income would be a bonus. Robin and I planned ahead for the costs to open a restaurant.

We had one hundred thirty thousand dollars available, which included our entire savings account, cashing in my 401K, taking out equity from our house, and borrowing money from her father. The personal loan was for working capital.

We wanted to lease space close to our home, so Robin and I prayed about it. We placed our faith on Proverbs 3:5 and 6 "Trust in the Lord with all your heart: do not depend on your own understanding. Seek His will in all you do, and He will show you which path to take." We quickly found out that the storefronts that we could afford were too far away from our home. During our search for a place to lease Robin befriended a woman named Carla. She had just opened a flower shop in a small strip mall located in downtown Chula Vista, about two miles from our home.

During one of their conversations Carla said to Robin that the pizza place, just two doors down from her shop, was coming available. It was a well-known national chain. The square footage was about what we were looking for. It faced Main Street and was directly across from a large mall. Since the pizza place was under the same management as Carla's shop, Robin asked her to let the property owner know that she was interested. Robin and I thought that it was strange for a well-known pizza chain to close its doors on a very busy street. We didn't want to get our hopes up just yet because maybe the rent would be too high but we couldn't stop thinking that maybe God planned ahead of time for us to have it.

Within two weeks the storefront was vacated and a lease sign was put up. Because the economy in early 2001 was on a decline the space may not have been leased right away but Robin and I wanted to act on it right away. If it was God's plan for us to open a restaurant there we didn't want to miss the opportunity by being late. Robin went to visit Carla to talk about the available storefront. Shortly after Robin got there the property owner (George) walked in. Robin and I do not believe in coincidences. We believe in God's timing. After Robin was introduced to George she mentioned to him that we were interested in leasing the vacant storefront. He said, "Contact the real estate office that I hired." Robin replied, "Maybe we could work something out without a realtor" but George said it was too late for that.

Robin then drove home and called the real estate number right away and asked what the lease was going for. It was within our budget! She set up an appointment for the two of us to see it later that day. Once inside Robin and I tried not to show too much excitement because we didn't want to give away our upper hand for negotiation. We knew it was perfect! Robin couldn't hold the excitement any longer and blurted out, "This is our building! God is going to give it to us!" The real estate agent said, "You are Christians? So am I." Right then Robin and I knew for sure that God was making a way for us to have the space. We then filled out the lease application right there in the storefront.

Because C&M Custom Party Planners was run from our home the business didn't have to pay rent. That was a good thing for us but not for a commercial lease application. A credit history was required but there wasn't any, not even a credit card in the business' name. We also didn't have enough income to be approved for the lease. The only income we had to show was what the catering business was making. Robin's father said that he would cosign the lease.

We asked the property owner for a five-year lease, a lower monthly rental amount, the first six months' rent free, no rent increase for three years and we did not want to pay first and last month's rent upfront. We had to wait three days before hearing back, which seemed to take forever. The owner counter offered. He said that there was another business interested in the space but he wanted us to have it if we could make it work. Robin did make a good impression when they first met in Carla's flower shop. George agreed to some of our terms. We had to pay the first and last month rent upfront and only three free months instead of six. That worked for us! A few days before February Robin and I received keys to our storefront. I thought, "We are on our way to financial success!" The first week of January 2001 I gave a thirty-day notice at RJD. We also decided to change our name. When we opened our doors, we would be Croom's Catering & BBQ!

Each day Robin and I woke up early with hope and anticipation of good things to come. We were excited about what God had done for us. The two of us took daily walks and talked about the many possibilities that our new venture would bring. We sang songs praising Jesus!

Robin and I budgeted our personal and business expenses for the following twelve months. We figured out a way for the one hundred thirty thousand dollar nest-egg to sustain us during that time. We thought the business would turn a profit by the end of the year to not only support the restaurant but our personal expenses, too.

Our understanding of getting a permit to operate a restaurant was that a health inspector would check out our commercial space to see that everything was up to code, clean, and in working order. Robin and I thought, "No problem it will be quick and simple. We will be open for business and making money in no time." But it didn't happen like that. The well-known proverbial expression "the best laid plans of mice and men often go awry" was to rear its head in our planning scenario.

The restaurant had a kitchen, one restroom for the employees to use, and a small dining room, but no office space. So, Robin asked her brother, Wayne, if he would build an office in the dining area just off the kitchen. Wayne, being skilled in construction, said he would do anything to help us become a success. To our surprise, while no one was at our storefront a health inspector came unannounced. He looked through the window and saw that the office space was framed and two by fours scattered on the floor. He then he left a notice on our door saying that we needed to re-apply for a use permit. We didn't know that if the inner structure was being changed we needed to put that in our permit application. Robin and I didn't let that spoil our excitement of opening a restaurant; we re-applied.

God gave us the vision, he confirmed it in our hearts, he blessed us with a perfect location, and he made a way for us to have a generous nest-egg until we were up and running. What more could we ask for? We were on course and everything was perfect! At this time, we never imagined the tremendous trial that was about to come, we were just overwhelmed and excited about what God was going to do.

When the health inspector came out for the second time the office was completed, everything was in operating order and clean. Instead of a quick and easy use permit being granted, we received a very long list of things that needed to be taken care of beforehand. It was mind boggling to say the least. Robin and I were in complete shock as the inspector led us to every area of our restaurant explaining the many changes that we would have to make. For starters, the hood that the pizza business was using was a different type than the hood that was required for our restaurant. We also learned that a fire suppressant system was needed in addition to our new hood. Next was the walk-in refrigerator. The inspector said because there were chips in the concrete floor it needed to be resurfaced and painted. Robin and I were getting very frustrated. Then we were led to the scullery area and were informed that we didn't have the proper sink system. A combined three-sink (dishwashing) system and a separate food prep sink had to be installed. Another required change included a new grease trap because the one we had wasn't up to code. By the time the inspector was done Robin and I were numb and just about speechless. When the inspector was done showing us everything that needed to be changed he handed us the list and said, "Call me to reschedule when you get everything on the list completed. Have a nice day." Robin asked if he had references to give us for a contractor to do the work and he said, "No, I'm not allowed to do that."

Robin and I couldn't believe what just happened. She got discouraged and started to cry. Neither of us knew anything about hoods, flooring, sink systems and grease traps, etc. I said to her, "Don't worry. When we pray we don't worry because it is in God's hands. We have enough money to get this stuff done and we will have a small nest-egg left for our cushion." Robin felt a little better after that. If only we could have done without an office!

We got right to it by opening the Yellow Pages to look for contractors. Since this process was new to us we asked other restaurant owners in our area for advice and we prayed a lot. We quickly learned that plans had to be drawn up for a new hood and fire suppression system, which required a building permit. Robin and I had no idea how to do that but God led us to a knowledgeable and professional contractor who drew up the plans at no extra cost. Normally when permits have to be pulled from the city it is a long process, but God made a way for us to get everything done within a couple of months!

Chapter 13

Depression

(Robin)

Lance and I received the keys to our brand new business space in February of 2001, but we did not open until May of that same year. The changes that had to be made proved to be a grueling process but with the Lord's help we got it all done. After completing all the necessary requirements to get the restaurant opened our "cushion" was gone! All the money that we had budgeted to sustain us for a year was used up within two months. As I look back I realize our faith was being tested. God did not want our dependence to be on the money we had, he wanted our dependence to be on him. It was an uncomfortable space to be in. How would we pay all our bills? Our safety net had been taken away and the full magnitude of Lance quitting his job and us starting up a brand new business hit us full force. What had we done? What were we thinking? Our oldest son, Karama, was due to graduate from Morehouse College in May and we had promised him a job in the business, but how would we be able to pay him? Those questions haunted our faith, but what I didn't know was that my faith would be tested even more.

Lance and I worked real hard and long hours to make the business a success, but the customers were not coming through the doors as quickly and frequently as we thought they would. We didn't realize it would take time to build up a customer base. As the days went by and the cash register showed less than desirable results at the end of the day, the anxiety within Lance began to build. I could tell Lance was becoming uneasy with the outcome of all our hard work.

Depression wasn't a concept that I was familiar with. Yes, there were days that I was a little down in the dumps, and even days that I didn't want to get out of bed, but true depression I was not familiar with. Since Lance started acting differently and his moods and behaviors started becoming inconsistent with who I knew Lance to be, I became concerned. I didn't know what was happening, but I knew something was seriously wrong. There are a lot of misconceptions about depression. I have even heard people say, "just snap out of it" or "everyone has problems, get over it" or how about this one, "how can a Christian be depressed?" Through my experience and research, I found out that depression is a very serious condition and there are many reasons or even a combination of reasons why a person might become depressed. These include traumatic life experiences such as the death of a loved one, certain diseases or medicines, substance abuse, hormonal changes, or a family history of depression. Sometimes the cause of depression is unknown. Lance and I had undertaken a major change in our life. Although it was a change that was directed by God, it was a change that would be the catalyst that triggered Lance's depression. Later, you will get a greater understanding of what was going on within Lance's mind.

I learned that whatever the circumstances, depression is caused by an imbalance of certain chemicals in the brain. Normally, these "chemical messengers" help nerve cells communicate with one another by sending and receiving messages. They may also influence a person's mood. In the case of depression, the available supply of the chemical messengers is low, so nerve cells can't communicate effectively. This often results in symptoms of depression. Anyone, regardless of age, gender, race, or socioeconomic status, can suffer from depression. Depression is not a weakness or a character flaw—it is a real medical illness!

Every day Lance seemed to struggle with the ordinary, familiar things of our life. He started having doubts about leaving his career. More and more I would hear him say that he wanted to go back to his job and that I could run the business with my son. Lance was uneasy and the joy that once exuded from him turned to sadness and unhappiness. I didn't know what to do! Why did he want to go back? Didn't he understand that God had told him to leave? I felt like him wanting to go back was like the Israelites wanting to go back to Egypt. It would be a lack of faith and I didn't want him to go back. As the days went by I could see Lance's countenance become darker, his feelings, thoughts and behaviors were changing, and I couldn't do anything to stop it. I prayed and prayed and the answer came after talking to my pastor's wife. God said, "Let him go back." I didn't understand at the time, but I came to understand that this was Lance's journey and he had to go through the valley. I knew that God was in the valley as well so I told Lance that he had my support and it was okay for him to go back to work and Karama and I could run the restaurant. It wasn't that I was making the decision for him, we just needed to be on one accord, and God made sure we were.

The Department of Corrections reinstated Lance back into his former position, so he went back to work. Little did we know, but his going back to work would not solve the depression that he had already begun to suffer. Once the enemy gets his hands on you he is not going to let go without a fight!

The purpose of going back to work was to regain the security and "cushion" that we had given up, but it didn't turn out the way that he thought it would. Going back didn't solve the problem it just created new ones. Upon re-entering the land that he had left, Lance took the depression with him, and depression took some his friends. Along with depression came uncertainty, irritability, restlessness, constant fatigue, loss of energy, feelings of worthlessness, difficulty concentrating, and difficulty in making decisions. I recall the day when I got a frantic call from Lance from his job. There had been an incident with an inmate who cut his wrist and drew pentagrams on the walls of his cell with his blood. Lance was called to respond to the incident then write a report. This was one of his work responsibilities that he had done hundreds of times before, however this time he was unable to do his job. The incident pushed him over the edge and because his blood pressure went through the roof, an ambulance was called and he was taken to the emergency room. His doctor put him off work which brought some relief to Lance, but the depression continued.

During the time of Lance's depressed state, I was also dealing with the sickness of my brother that I spoke of in chapter two. Sometimes when it rains, it pours! God was taking this test to another level! I've come to understand now why God allows us to go through trials, he wants us to be complete in Him. God was preparing me through the trials and sorrows of life. Preparing me for what my eventual calling would be.

On September 11, 2001 the terrible news of the attacks on the World Trade Center filled the morning news and the nation was devastated. I didn't know at the time that our family would be devastated by another event. Later that day I got a call from my sister-in-law, Donna. She said that my brother was back in the hospital and we should come up and see him. I didn't think that it was critical because since his lung transplant he had been in and out of the hospital many times. I decided to wait until the weekend to go. That night as I slept, the Lord sent my earthly father to me in a dream to tell me I couldn't wait to go see Craig, that I needed to go immediately. When I awoke the next morning there was an urgency not only for me to go, but for me to tell the whole family to go. On Wednesday, September 12, 2001, Lance and I drove on a deserted freeway from San Diego to the UCLA Medical Center in Los Angeles. It was an eerie drive since no planes were in the sky and very few cars were on the road.

As the whole family converged in the hospital to be with Craig, no one knew that on that day our beloved Craig would die. I believe he knew because he had final words to share with each of us. One of the last memories that I have of my brother was to witness the internal strength that he possessed. At that time his lungs were failing and he was on full oxygen. He could barely breathe, but he refused to use a bedpan. I watched as he got out of his bed, walked to the bathroom that was in his room, and walked back to his bed. By the time he got back into his bed he was gasping for air. I watched determination in action! Soon afterwards Craig had to be intubated and never regained consciousness again. My brother was taken off life support after an agonizing decision by his wife, and he died within the hour. I thank God for His love and compassion for me and my family. Had we not gone when we did, we would not have had the opportunity to see Craig that one last time! I learned to listen to God when he speaks to me and then do what he says! Always trust and obey!

Dealing with a severely depressed husband, grieving the death of my baby brother, and having to run a business that was on life support was more than a notion. A catering event (wedding) was booked for that Sunday after my brother died so I had no time to "fall apart." On Saturday, the evening before the wedding, I told Lance we needed to go to the restaurant to prepare. He told me to go ahead and he would join me in an hour. He seemed to be unusually tired so I decided to give him the extra time to rest. After the hour passed and he didn't come, I called to see where he was. No one answered the phone. I called several times before he answered. His voice was groggy. He asked me to come pick him up, which I did. When we got to the restaurant he went to the office and fell asleep. I had no time to try to get him to help me so I did the work myself. After I completed everything I went and got him from the office and we went home. The next morning, we got up and did the event. It was a total success and our customer was so satisfied with our work they gave us a big tip! When we got back to the restaurant to put the equipment away, Lance dropped a bombshell on me. He told me that he had tried to take his life by taking some pills the previous night. I was devastated but thankful at the same time. God had spared his life! Monday was our day off so I dealt with all the details of planning for my brother's home going service. I didn't get a break! It was one challenge to the next. On Tuesday it was time to go back to work. I was near the front of the restaurant when Lance said these words to me;

"You never lost your faith. Never give up, God will take care of you."

When he said that to me my thoughts went back to the weekend when he had tried to take his life. I was so overwhelmed! For months I was holding on to everything I knew of God, His character and His promises, but I was so exhausted! Physically, spiritually, emotionally, I was tapped out. I had nothing left in me to continue to fight. I shouted at him.

"Don't say that to me!"

At that moment all energy left my body and I collapsed. Lance caught me and carried me to the office. My sister-in-law (Tory) was there and I could hear her say,

"Oh no, not Robin too."

I could hear Lance say,

"Robin, I'm sorry, it's going to be ok. Please Robin, please don't leave me."

I felt like life was seeping from my body. It felt like a falling away, a spiraling down. I could hear everything that was being said, but I could not respond verbally or physically. At some point of falling away, I heard a voice say, "if you leave, what is going to happen to your husband?" All of a sudden I felt the presence of something pushing me back, stopping the spiraling down. Lance carried me to the car to take me home; at the same time a friend from church was on her way to see me. She caught me just before Lance pulled away. She opened the door and pressed her body to mine in a hug. It felt like energy was being transferred from her body into mine. I started to feel like life and strength was being infused into my body. Still I hadn't spoken. Lance took me home where I fell asleep for five hours. When I awoke I felt better, but it seemed like my life was shattered and broken. I was tired and I felt alone! Where was He? Why was He allowing us to go through all this? I hadn't heard His voice for months. My thoughts were "Lord, I need you, NOW!" Lance was concerned about me and he was in the room with me. The phone rang. My son brought the phone to us, but I told him I didn't want to speak to anyone. Lance took the phone and by the conversation on his end I could tell he was talking to our pastor. I had enlisted his prayers many months before. I could tell our pastor had asked him if he was okay and how he was doing because Lance said, "Yeah, I'm fine."

NO, NO! I crawled across the bed and took the phone from Lance's hands. I said,

"Pastor, he is not okay, he tried to kill himself!"

My pastor said many things to me that night, but the only thing I remember him saying was, "Robin it's going to be okay!" And it seemed like it was the voice of God! I heard it and it provided some comfort in the midst of the storm.

The next day, when I was all alone, all the frustration, confusion, heartache, fatigue, loneliness and sorrow came out in my cry to the Lord. The tears were flowing and my nose was running. I was at the end of myself with no answers. I had to hear from God! The following words came out of my mouth in total surrender to the One who had the answers that I needed.

I don't understand Lord! *How can you give us a ministry that takes both of us and how can you give us a vision for this business, then take my husband away from me?* I don't understand! *I don't want my testimony to be how to get over losing your spouse,* I DON'T WANT THAT TO BE MY TESTIMONY LORD! *But, I'm not telling you what to do.*

Suddenly, a calm resolve came over me, and the next words out of my mouth were...

But, whatever road I have to travel, I will go. And whatever path I have to take, I will take it. I will serve you Lord! I will praise you Lord, and I will continue to love you Lord!

It was at this point of total surrender to my sovereign God, relinquishing my will for his good, perfect and acceptable will, that I heard the loving voice of God! He said these words to me...

"Robin, that is not going to be your testimony, I'm just working with him" (speaking of my husband Lance).

The tears continued to flow, but I was so thankful that God spoke to me and let me know (without any doubt) that my husband would be okay. The next item on the agenda was to quickly go and share with Lance the word that I had gotten from God.

Lance heeded my words, but he did not come out of the depression immediately. It took another few months, but when he did, it was like Lazarus coming up out of the grave. Lance was on fire for the Lord and our life was on smooth waters once again. Lance and I were closer than ever before and our ministry was going strong. Everything seemed to be back in order.

As the years passed something unexpected happened. Lance experienced a second episode of depression. This time he went deeper and stayed longer than the first time. I didn't understand what was happening. Having gone through this once before, I was a lot stronger this time around however I constantly asked God why this was happening again. I got no answers from God except Him telling me that what he had told me before still stood. "He was working with Lance." Why couldn't God do everything he needed to do in Lance the first time? Why allow us to go through this again? God would not answer those questions either, but in no uncertain terms God told me to leave Lance to him and do what he had called me to do. When our ministry with marriage had been put on hold during the first depression episode, God had called me to a ministry with women. I began to pour myself into developing a bible-study for women that would focus on the issues that women deal with on a daily basis and how to apply the word of God in a practical way to become victorious in life. In hind-sight (which is 20/20) I understand God was developing me at the same time he was developing Lance. All I could do was trust God, be patient and keep moving forward doing the work of the Lord!

Chapter 14

Freedom

(Lance)

Through the many years of being with Robin, all the ups and downs, the trials and challenges, I came to trust her implicitly, even though sometimes she could be painfully honest. When she came to me to let me know that God had spoken to her, I listened intently to what she was saying. She told me that God was working with me and that I would be okay. That was enough to give me hope, to give me a dim light on which I could focus. I remember making statements in the past concerning people who wanted to commit suicide. I would say that they were weak and cowardly. I didn't understand until I had to face it myself. Depression is more than a mental problem; it is spiritual too. Demonic influences plagued my mind and soul. The spirit of heaviness weighed upon me and kept me bound. The enemy of my soul wanted to kill me and he used my past to do it. My faith was being tested and I didn't understand what was going on. It was only by the grace of God and his love that I got a better understanding of why I was depressed, even though I had to go through one more episode.

James 1:2-8 says. *"Dear brothers and sisters, when troubles of any kind come your way, consider it an opportunity for great joy. For you know that when your faith is tested, your endurance has a chance to grow. So let it grow, for when your endurance is fully developed, you will be perfect and complete, needing nothing. If you need wisdom, ask our generous God, and he will give it to you. He will not rebuke you for asking. But when you ask him, be sure that your faith is in God alone. Do not waver, for a person with divided loyalty is as unsettled as a wave of the sea that is blown and tossed by the wind. Such people should not expect to receive anything from the Lord. Their loyalty is divided between God and the world, and they are unstable in everything they do."*

Once I came up out of the depression, I ask God WHY? God showed me that it had started when I was a young child, living in the depressing inner city of Detroit. I didn't realize how much the events of my childhood and all the bad things that I did played a big role in why I became depressed. As I stated earlier in chapter one, I vowed as a four-year-old child that I would do better if I had the chance. Also I did terrible things as a child that I buried deep in my conscience. I remember hearing members of my family saying that I was a bad child, but I also remember my mom saying "there are not bad children, there is bad parenting." The devil used my past against me and all I could remember was "I was a bad child!" When we began to struggle in the business, the thought of not having enough money to take care of my family plagued my soul. God showed me it was the fear of a young child that manifested in me as a grown man. Fear of lack and poverty. Once the fear took hold of me it wasn't long before I lost all perspective. Then everything that I had done as a young child/youth, the enemy brought back to my remembrance.

Having a depressed state of mind, I couldn't differentiate between real and fiction. Was I bad? Could everything I had done as a child keep me from the love of God? The word of God that I loved became the hammer of justice that pushed me deeper into the abyss of hopelessness. I knew God and I knew that I belonged to Him, but the knowledge was a head knowledge, not a heart knowledge. The scriptures tell us in Romans 10:9-10 that *"If you openly declare that Jesus is Lord and believe in your heart that God raised him from the dead, you will be saved. For it is by believing in your heart that you are made right with God, and it is by openly declaring your faith that you are saved."*

I had confessed with my mouth that Jesus died for my sins, but Romans 8 hadn't settled in my heart.

Romans 8:28-39 says. *"And we know that God causes everything to work together for the good of those who love God and are called according to his purpose for them. For God knew his people in advance, and he chose them to become like his Son, so that his Son would be the firstborn among many brothers and sisters. And having chosen them, he called them to come to him. And having called them, he gave them right standing with himself. And having given them right standing, he gave them his glory. What shall we say about such wonderful things as these? If God is for us, who can ever be against us? Since he did not spare even his own Son but gave him up for us all, won't he also give us everything else? Who dares accuse us whom God has chosen for his own? No one, for God himself has given us right standing with himself. Who then will condemn us? No one, for Christ Jesus died for us and was raised to life for us, and he is sitting in the place of honor at God's right hand, pleading for us. Can anything ever separate us from Christ's love? Does it mean he no longer loves us if we have trouble or calamity, or are persecuted, or hungry, or destitute, or in danger, or threatened with death? As the scriptures say, "for your sake we are killed every day; we are being slaughtered like sheep." No, despite all these things, overwhelming victory is ours through Christ, who loved us. And I am convinced that nothing can ever separate us from God's love. Neither death nor life, neither angels nor demons, neither our fears for today nor our worries about tomorrow, not even the powers of hell can separate us from God's love. No power in the sky above or in the earth below; indeed, nothing in all creation will ever be able to separate us from the love of God that is revealed in Christ Jesus our Lord."*

As this scripture settled in my heart, the devil lost all leverage against me. When Robin asked me how I knew I wouldn't succumb to depression again, I told her what God had revealed to me. When I came out of the depression the first time, the root cause had not been revealed and through time the root of the depression grew again. You have to seek God for the root cause, bring it to the light, then face your demons with courage. Pull that thing up from the root and it cannot grow again! When God frees you, you are truly FREE! I pray that this scripture will free you too!

Chapter 15

Where We Are Now

(Robin)

So, I know you are wondering where are we now? What are we doing and how did everything turn out? This is not the typical happily-ever-after ending that you see in fairy tales, but it does end well! Lance never returned to the department of corrections. After fifteen years of operating our restaurant, we closed the doors in 2014, but continue our catering business to this day. We are just a regular married couple that have moments of intense fellowship, argue at times, and struggle with the issues of life, just like you do. As long as we live on this side of heaven we will experience many trials and many sorrows, BUT because Jesus overcame it all; even in death we can experience abundant life. When you are on the battlefield you will experience heartache, sorrows, challenges, and failures. But, if you continue to trust in God and keep the faith, you can experience joy, peace, and contentment. You will be victorious!

Lance and I have been to hell and back. We have experienced things that neither one of us could have contemplated. We have overcome tough obstacles and have weathered some pretty raging storms, and we have survived! We have learned many lessons on this journey. We know that there is nothing more fulfilling than giving our WHOLE heart to the Lord and trusting him with it. *"We know that all things do work together for good, for those who love God, for those who are called according to His purpose."* We know that we were destined to be together and will be together until "death do us part!" Lance, recalling a Smokey Robinson song would say; "it would be easier to separate wet from water, all the dry from sand, than for anyone to try to separate us, keep us from holding hands..." It's hard to mention Lance without mentioning Robin, and vice versa.

We recognize that we cannot change one another, so we stopped trying. We accept each other unconditionally, understanding that if we have an issue with the other, we can take it to the Lord in prayer. God resolves all issues. We love and respect each other and we have each other's back. Team Croom has always been unbeatable. The team consists of Lance, me, and the Lord up above! He is our captain, our encourager, our protector, our redeemer, and our friend. But most of all he is our Savior and Lord!

Both Lance and I are pastors awaiting the green light to plant our first church. Until then we keep busy by sharing our faith with others through personal mentoring, bible studies, planning marriage conferences, and sharing our story around the world. We are planning our first mission trip to Africa to help strengthen marriages through seminars and conferences. People need to see that we can have happy, wholesome, victorious marriages. We can raise happy, healthy children. We can be a model of a Christ-centered marriage.

From our three children, we have six wonderful grandchildren that keep us pretty busy. Five grandsons and one granddaughter. Our life is full of adventure and love. We are a close family and since we all live in the same city, we frequently have family gatherings.

We started this book over four and a half years ago. The devil did not want to see it finished. He wanted this book to die on the vine and be buried in an early grave, and he gave it his best effort. But God had a different plan when he breathed the title into my soul those many years ago. I remember one of Lance's sermons that tells the story of the eagle, the only bird that doesn't take refuge in the midst of a storm. As I reflect on that sermon I am convinced that God carried us through our storms of life, and we want you to know that if you wait upon the Lord, you can mount up as on wings of eagles too. God may not take you out of your stormy season, but He will see you through and keep you in His perfect peace if you trust Him. You will not be overtaken so buckle up and hold on to His hand! God is able! God Bless, be encouraged!

Chapter 16

God Encounters

We want to share the following stories with you that helped shape our lives. We call them encounters with God. We hope they inspire and encourage you on your journey.

Story #1

Preparation For The Storm

(Robin)

In 1998, after our son's first year at Morehouse College, the whole family took a bus trip from California to Georgia to help pack up his dorm room and store his possessions at the home of good friends of my parents. They lived in a beautiful remote area with the backyard having a lake so close you could sit on the upper balcony and fish in the lake. On the day that Lance, I, and our daughter Toni went to the dorms to help Karama pack up, my son Kashif and my mom and dad stayed at their friend's home. Kashif stayed because he wanted to fish. We were gone the better part of the day and when we arrived back to the house I ask my parents where Kashif was. They told me they thought he was with us! Well there was a communication error that day because we thought they knew he had stayed at the house to fish. To make matters drastically worse, Kashif was nowhere to be found. We all scoured the forty-five hundred square foot home. We looked in every room, upstairs and downstairs. We looked in the basement and all around the neighborhood. It was starting to get dark and my nerves started to get rattled. Anxiety started to grow inside of me and I couldn't stay out of the bathroom! Lance got into the car and drove around the neighborhood and we called in a missing person's report. The neighbors took out their flashlights and helped us to look for our son. As the night got darker, my stomach turned over and over. My mind became active and I started imagining the worst scenarios about where my son could be. In desperation I went to the bathroom for the third time, but this time I looked myself in the mirror and started praying to God. I said, "I know you know where my son is and I need you to show me where he is. Please keep him safe from all harm and danger. I don't know what else to do but come to you." At this point I could not get any comfort from my parents or my husband. Everyone was as frantic as I was. All of a sudden, as if on auto-pilot, I left the bathroom and walked down the stairs to the basement (which I had been to twice before). I walked past the sofa and chairs, past the pool table and straight to the closet. When I opened the closet I saw my baby boy fast asleep on the closet floor! What a relief. I didn't even wake him up, I just ran fast as I could to tell the others that I had found him! Later that night the Lord spoke to me. He said, "Robin, you need to know that a day will come that you will have no one to lean on but me. You will have to trust me completely." I didn't understand then but I do now, completely. God prepares us for the things that we will encounter in life, we just don't know that he is doing it at the time. Is God preparing you?

Story #2

The Voice Of God

(Lance)

The year was 1997 and I had been praying about recognizing the voice of God. I wanted to know when God was speaking to me. On one beautiful sunny day in San Diego, God would answer my prayer. I was leaving the tennis courts to meet up with my family at a local restaurant. I was already running late so my focus was on getting to the restaurant as soon as I could. As I was driving up the street I passed a man standing at a bus stop. I heard a voice within me say "stop and ask him if he needs a ride." Because I was running late I decided to keep driving. I then heard the voice again say "go back and ask him if he needs a ride." I weighed the choice to continue on or to go back and do as the voice within had instructed. I chose to go back. I made a u-turn and went back, even though I would be even later reaching my destination. When I reached the man at the bus-stop I asked him if he needed a ride. The words of his reply will stay with me forever. He said "No, I don't need a ride, but you were just being obedient to the Holy Spirit, now be on your way!" Wow, what a practical demonstration from God. As I started driving I looked into my rear-view mirror and the man waiting at the bus-stop was GONE! Was that an angel on assignment by God to answer my prayer? Many may ponder in their minds what really happened on that sunny day, but I know in my spirit that what I experienced was an encounter with God!

Story #3

In The Arms Of Jesus

(Robin)

It was 1984 and I was pregnant with my youngest son. This was a difficult time in my life because Lance was in the world doing the things of the world. It wasn't unusual for Lance not to come home from work because the drug cocaine had his full attention. I didn't know what to do and I had no one to talk to. How could I let anyone know what my husband was doing? I held all the pain, worry, and disappointment inside of me. One night as I was waiting for him to come home I broke down in a fit of tears. I couldn't take it anymore. I sat huddled in the corner of my sunken living room, alone. As despair overtook me and my tears soaked my clothing, I felt a pair of arms wrap around me. I had no way of explaining it because I was home alone. As I was being held a total peace washed over my body and I stopped crying. I didn't know what was happening but I felt safe and secure. A few minutes later my doorbell rang and when I opened the door Lance's brother Michael was standing before me. All the pain and hurt came out of me as I shared with Michael what was going on in my life. He didn't have the answers or the solution but sharing my struggle with him did lift a burden from my heart. At the time I couldn't explain what happened, but somehow I knew that God had visited me, wrapped me in His arms and let me know that He had me. Now I know for certain that what I experienced that lonely night was a "God Encounter." God will never leave his children alone; neither will He abandon them. Hebrews 13:5 (paraphrased)

Story #4

Answered Prayer

(Lance)

The question is asked, what is faith? Hebrews 11:1 states that faith is the substance of things hoped for and the evidence of things not seen. More simply stated for me it means trusting God regardless of your current circumstances. I have so many stories that proved to me that God is a rewarder of those who would diligently seek Him. One of my favorites took place in December 1997. My oldest son Karama Croom was a senior in high school and due to graduate in May of the upcoming year. He was planning to attend Morehouse College in the fall of that same year. The entire family was excited about the prospect of him attending Morehouse that fall. One evening his mother and I were discussing our finances and trying to figure out how we would pay for his tuition and room and board for the next four years. My wife's father and mother, Henry and Sylvia Mitchell, had set aside a substantial amount of money to help with their grandsons' education. His mother and I also came up with a part of the finances that were needed. As we were crunching numbers we discovered that we only had half the amount that it would take to support him over the next four years. We went over the numbers several times and received the same results. We were still only half way to the amount of money needed to put him through college. As our frustration begin to mount, I was reminded by the Holy Spirit that we had not prayed. I told my wife, we've done all that we can do, let's pray and ask God for his help with our situation. I began to pray and during my prayer our home phone began to ring. Normally I would have allowed the answering machine to catch the call but I felt for some reason I needed to take this call. I stopped and answered the phone. The voice on the other end of the phone said, "Is this Mr. Croom, the father of Karama Croom?" I said yes it is, the gentleman stated his name, Dr. Long, and that he was the president of the Alumni Association from Morehouse College. He stated that he had a half tuition academic scholarship for my son to attend Morehouse College. As the tears began to flow, I began to shout thank you Jesus thank you Lord thank you Jesus thank you Lord. You cannot tell me that God is not real.

Story #5

A Call To Obedience

(Robin)

After God called me into the ministry for women it seemed like all hell broke loose. It was one test after another and they all involved women! One intense test in particular would forever change how I would respond to God's future request of me. I got a phone call from a friend of mine. She said that someone had spoken an untruth about me concerning confidentiality in ministry. I was hurt and confused as to why someone would say that about me. I asked my friend if she would tell me who had said it, but she was uncomfortable in revealing her source. I went to the Lord and prayed about the situation. I let God know how hurt I was and asked him why someone would say that. I also asked God to tell me who had spoken the untrue statements. The following Sunday while worshipping in church the Lord showed me exactly who had spoken against me. It was like a laser beam pointed out this woman standing in the pulpit area. I knew in my spirit that God had answered my prayer, but what was I to do with this newfound information? Weeks passed and bitterness towards this woman began to build up in my heart. I felt like she was a hypocrite. Smiling in my face, lifting her arms in praise and worship, but secretly talking behind my back. What made matters worse was that I thought she was my friend! The Sunday finally came when I couldn't praise or worship because my spirit was so heavy. The Lord told me to ask this woman to pray with me. As we walked to the prayer room of our church my heart towards her started to soften. As we seated ourselves across from each other I opened the conversation by saying, "it seems like there is a wall up between us, if there is anything that I have done to offend or hurt you I'm sorry. I would do nothing to intentionally hurt you, I love you." Her response surprised me. She told me of a time when I had given her some advice that had offended her. She further stated that I had been nothing but a friend to her. She stated that it was her loss and she was sorry for being so stand-off-ish. I never did divulge that I knew what she had said about me, but I did talk to her about the tricks and schemes of the enemy. I talked about how Satan wants to separate us women with the lie that we cannot get along, and so many other untruths to keep us from trusting one another. We prayed together, hugged and I thought that everything had been resolved that day in our prayer room. As the days and weeks passed by I noticed that she continued to avoid me. If I came in one door of the church she would go out a different door, anything to avoid me. When she had no choice but to interact with me I got the perfunctory smile and a dispassionate greeting. I really wanted to write her off, but God told me to "love her!" I told God that she didn't want to be friends with me and I really didn't want to be friends with her either. God was adamant. He asked me this question, "didn't you promise me that you would do what I ask of you?" What could I say to that? God said again, "love her." So I continued to be friendly and give her gifts and words of encouragement. I remember the day that I had made a basket of soaps and lotions for her (because God told me to do it). I brought it to church two Sundays in a row but didn't give it to her. My excuse was that I didn't see her. On the third Sunday God admonished me and told me to give it to her, I did. She smiled and accepted my gift but I didn't feel the love from her. To make a long story short, she eventually left our church and I didn't see her for two years. I thought of her often and wondered what she was doing. The funny thing about it all is I really did like her. As a matter of fact, she reminded me of myself in a lot of ways. Why had God asked me to "love her?" What was God trying to teach me? The answer to my question wasn't answered right away. Two years later I got a phone call from Shelley, a close friend and sister in Christ. She asked me if I wanted to attend a 6am prayer group with her. I really wasn't feeling getting up by 5am and traveling twenty-five minutes to attend a prayer group, but I knew God wanted me there, so I went. What a surprise I got when I saw this woman that I hadn't seen in two years, leading the prayer group! After several visits she ask if she could speak to me. This is what she said. "I want to thank you and let you know I got it!" I ask her "got what?" She continued, "I've never in my life experienced unconditional love from anyone, but I got that from you. You showed me something that I had never seen before and I want to say thank you for loving me. I know that I was difficult, so thank you." It was complete closure for me. God showed me why he asked me to love her. I didn't understand at the time, but I am so thankful that I was obedient even when I didn't want to be. God uses us to show his love for one another, and if we say we love God we will love each other. Love comes from God and flows through us! I haven't seen her since our final encounter, but I know for sure that God used me to heal the heart, the hurts and the past of this woman by a demonstration of his love! Bless God!

Lance (L), Norman (C), Gregory ®

Robin (first row, second from left)

Robin on train in homemade dress

Lance and Robin (Wedding 1977)

Still in love......

Made in the USA
Charleston, SC
26 June 2016